Writing the Critical Essay

Democracy

An OPPOSING VIEWPOINTS® Guide

Lauri S. Friedman, *Book Editor*

OPPOSING
VIEWPOINTS®
SERIES

GREENHAVEN PRESS
A part of Gale, Cengage Learning

GALE
CENGAGE Learning™

Detroit • New York • San Francisco • New Haven, Conn • Waterville, Maine • London

Christine Nasso, *Publisher*
Elizabeth Des Chenes, *Managing Editor*

For more information, contact:
Greenhaven Press
27500 Drake Rd.
Farmington Hills, MI 48331-3535
Or you can visit our Internet site at gale.cengage.com

For product information and technology assistance, contact us at

Gale Customer Support, 1-800-877-4253
For permission to use material from this text or product, submit all requests online at
www.cengage.com/permissions

Further permissions questions can be emailed to permissionrequest@cengage.com

Articles in Greenhaven Press anthologies are often edited for length to meet page requirements. In addition, original titles of these works are changed to clearly present the main thesis and to explicitly indicate the author's opinion. Every effort is made to ensure that Greenhaven Press accurately reflects the original intent of the authors. Every effort has been made to trace the owners of copyrighted material.

Cover image © Scott Lomenzo, 2008. Used under license from Shutterstock.com

LIBRARY OF CONGRESS CATALOGING-IN-PUBLICATION DATA

Democracy / Lauri S. Friedman, book editor.
   p. cm. — (Writing the critical essay, an opposing viewpoints guide)
  Includes bibliographical references and index.
  ISBN 978-0-7377-4036-3 (hardcover)
  1. Democracy—United States. 2. War on Terrorism, 2001– 3. Terrorism. 4. Essay—Authorship—Problems, exercises, etc. I. Friedman, Lauri S.
  JK1726.D46 2008
  320.973—dc22

                         2008002153

Printed in the United States of America
1 2 3 4 5 6 7 12 11 10 09 08

CONTENTS

Examining the state of writing and how it is taught in the United States was the official purpose of the National Commission on Writing in America's Schools and Colleges. The commission, made up of teachers, school administrators, business leaders, and college and university presidents, released its first report in 2003. "Despite the best efforts of many educators," commissioners argued, "writing has not received the full attention it deserves." Among the findings of the commission was that most fourth-grade students spent less than three hours a week writing, that three-quarters of high school seniors never receive a writing assignment in their history or social studies classes, and that more than 50 percent of first-year students in college have problems writing error-free papers. The commission called for a "cultural sea change" that would increase the emphasis on writing for both elementary and secondary schools. These conclusions have made some educators realize that writing must be emphasized in the curriculum. As colleges are demanding an ever-higher level of writing proficiency from incoming students, schools must respond by making students more competent writers. In response to these concerns, the SAT, an influential standardized test used for college admissions, required an essay for the first time in 2005.

Books in the Writing the Critical Essay: An Opposing Viewpoints Guide series use the patented Opposing Viewpoints format to help students learn to organize ideas and arguments and to write essays using common critical writing techniques. Each book in the series focuses on a particular type of essay writing—including expository, persuasive, descriptive, and narrative—that students learn while being taught both the five-paragraph essay as well as longer pieces of writing that have an opinionated focus. These guides include everything necessary to help students research, outline, draft, edit, and ultimately write successful essays across the curriculum, including essays for the SAT.

Using Opposing Viewpoints

This series is inspired by and builds upon Greenhaven Press's acclaimed Opposing Viewpoints series. As in the parent series, each book in the Writing the Critical Essay series focuses on a timely and controversial social issue that provides lots of opportunities for creating thought-provoking essays. The first section of each volume begins with a brief introductory essay that provides context for the opposing viewpoints that follow. These articles are chosen for their accessibility and clearly stated views. The thesis of each article is made explicit in the article's title and is accentuated by its pairing with an opposing or alternative view. These essays are both models of persuasive writing techniques and valuable research material that students can mine to write their own informed essays. Guided reading and discussion questions help lead students to key ideas and writing techniques presented in the selections.

The second section of each book begins with a preface discussing the format of the essays and examining characteristics of the featured essay type. Model five-paragraph and longer essays then demonstrate that essay type. The essays are annotated so that key writing elements and techniques are pointed out to the student. Sequential, step-by-step exercises help students construct and refine thesis statements; organize material into outlines; analyze and try out writing techniques; write transitions, introductions, and conclusions; and incorporate quotations and other researched material. Ultimately, students construct their own compositions using the designated essay type.

The third section of each volume provides additional research material and writing prompts to help the student. Additional facts about the topic of the book serve as a convenient source of supporting material for essays. Other features help students go beyond the book for their research. Like other Greenhaven Press books, each book in the Writing the Critical Essay series includes bibliographic listings of relevant periodical articles, books, Web sites, and organizations to contact.

Writing the Critical Essay: An Opposing Viewpoints Guide will help students master essay techniques that can be used in any discipline.

The Challenges of Democracy

Most Americans regard democracy as the world's best political system. But what constitutes a democracy, and is the United States an example of a good one? According to the Economist Intelligence Unit (EIU), an organization that analyzes the world's governments, fully functioning democracies rank highly in each of the following categories: free elections, civil liberties, government functionality, political participation, and political culture. In other words, full, true democracies have free elections, and their citizens enjoy a high degree of civil liberties such as the right to privacy, speech, and assembly. Their governments function effectively and transparently, and their citizens embrace political issues and take opportunities to participate in the process.

According to the EIU's rankings, in 2007 Sweden was the most perfectly functioning democracy in the whole world. Sweden received perfect 10s in the categories of "electoral process and pluralism," "functioning of government," "political participation," and "civil liberties." Conversely, the United States ranked seventeenth, with many nations such as Denmark, Iceland, Norway, Australia, and Canada beating it for higher places in line. The EIU ranked the United States relatively low due to problems with the way its government functions and also due to low political participation in elections and debates. But seventeenth out of the 165 independent nations (and two territories) surveyed still places the United States as one of the strongest democracies in the entire world. Indeed, the United States is committed not only to preserving democracy within its borders, but encouraging the growth of democracy in other nations.

But while it is frequently championed by the United States and its allies, democracy has its own challenges

Free elections are one of the institutions that make the United States a successful democratic country.

and limitations that are important to explore. A main thrust behind the idea of democracy is that everyone has a say in the creation of their government and laws. Essentially, every person gets a voice, a vote. Of course, in a country such as the United States, with more than 300 million citizens, it would be impossible to poll every person on every issue. That is why representatives are elected to make decisions on behalf of the citizenry, and citizens restrict their voting to the election of those representatives (and sometimes on issues that are written directly on the ballot, called ballot initiatives, such as whether to increase funding for a specific project or to legalize gay marriage).

Though this democratic process attempts to give millions a say in the affairs of their country, it is important to realize that at the very same time, the process can leave thousands, even millions, with their political needs unmet. This is the flip side of majority rule—everyone has a vote, but not everyone may triumph in their vision for the country. For example, consider the fact that presidential elections usually come down to just a few percentage points, making the country essentially split between two candidates. In the 2004 election George W. Bush won 51 percent of the popular vote (with 62 million people in favor of him); his opponent, Democratic candidate John Kerry, had 48 percent of the vote (with 59 million people in favor of him). To say that Bush was the winner of the election is true, but the results clearly indicate he did not have the entire country's support; in fact, nearly half of the voting public turned out against him. In this way democracy often fails to serve the interests of all the people. This aspect of democracy was perhaps no better summed up than by a founder of American democracy, Thomas Jefferson. Indeed, Jefferson recognized the limitations of majority rule when he said, "A democracy is nothing more than mob rule, where fifty-one percent of the people may take away the rights of the other forty-nine."

Another inherent limitation of democracy is that it requires that the citizenry be informed so as to use their precious vote wisely. In other words, if citizens cast votes on issues that affect everyone, they had better be well aware of the pros, cons, consequences, and benefits of their actions. But too often Americans go to the polls uninformed about a particular candidate or ballot measure. Some vote along party lines without knowing much about the person for whom they are voting; still others vote arbitrarily, even picking people or ballot initiatives based on the sound of their name. Still others do not go at all, allowing the interests of those who do vote to trump the interests of the broader population.

The flip side of democracy is that not everyone's preferences may win in the end— such as in the 2004 presidential race between John Kerry and George W. Bush, in which nearly half the voting public voted against Bush for president.

Each of these circumstances can completely alter the outcome of an election, at times to society's detriment. Democracy in this form, then, appears more reckless than responsible, more frustrating than free and fair. As Winston Churchill once said of this facet of democracy, "The best argument against democracy is a five minute conversation with the average voter." In other words, if the average voter is uninformed on the issues, they will not be able to better society by participating in the democratic process, and may even put it at risk. Put another way by President John F. Kennedy, one of America's most beloved politicians and ardent champion of democracy: "The ignorance of one voter in a democracy impairs the security of all."

Being able to debate the positives and negatives of a democratic society, however, is evidence of its benefit. The freedom of speech, the freedom to assemble, and the freedom to vote in fair elections are rights that Americans have enjoyed in their democratic society for hundreds of years, despite the problems that come along with the system. The benefits and drawbacks of democracy are just a few of the issues explored in the articles and essays in *Writing the Critical Essay: An Opposing Viewpoints Guide: Democracy*. Model essays and viewpoints expose readers to the basic arguments made about democracy in today's world and help them develop tools to craft their own essays on the subject.

Section One: Opposing Viewpoints on Democracy

American Democracy Is Threatened by the War on Terror

Nicole Colson

In the following essay author Nicole Colson warns that the war on terror threatens American democracy. She explains several aspects of the war on terror that have reduced or violated the rights of American citizens. First she argues that the Patriot Act—passed after September 11 to help law enforcement catch terrorists—unconstitutionally violates the right to privacy. Under the act, innocent Americans may have their homes searched or have private medical or financial records scrutinized without their knowledge. The Patriot Act also threatens the democratic right to assemble; Colson tells of protestors who have been labeled as terrorists because of political slogans on their T-shirts. American freedom and democracy are under threat, warns Colson, not from terrorism, but from those who claim to protect against it.

Colson is a reporter for the *Socialist Worker,* where this essay originally was published. Her articles have also appeared on Counterpunch.org and in the *International Socialist Review.*

Consider the following questions:

1. What groups are among those viewed by the Defense Department as possible threats to national security, according to Colson?
2. What does Colson say Section 213 of the Patriot Act allows authorities to do?
3. Who is Tariq Ramadan, and how does his story support Colson's argument?

Nicole Colson, "Big Brother Is Watching You," *Socialist Worker,* January 27, 2006. Reproduced by permission.

Secret surveillance labeling peaceful protesters "threats" to national security, detaining immigrants for weeks and sometimes months—in the name of protecting freedom and democracy. It may sound like something out of a novel by Franz Kafka, but it's the reality of the Bush administration's war on our rights.

A War on American Liberties

Washington has been rocked by the recent *New York Times* revelations that George Bush signed a secret order in 2002 allowing the National Security Agency (NSA) to listen in on phone conversations and view e-mail messages of "hundreds, perhaps thousands" of people inside the U.S.—without a warrant.

Many people believe the USA PATRIOT Act threatens democracy because it allows constitutional rights to be violated in the name of fighting terrorism.

Coming on top of revelations that the Defense Department has a 400-page list of hundreds of groups and protests that it considered possible "threats" to national security—including a Quaker group and student antiwar demonstrations against military recruitment held on at least eight college campuses—it's clear that the Bush administration has taken its attack on our civil liberties to unprecedented new levels.

This week, the administration is stepping up its drive to win reauthorization of the USA PATRIOT Act—the post–September 11 law that set much of the attack on our rights in motion.

From the first days after September 11, the government set out to expand its ability to spy, detain and prosecute—and now the Bush administration wants measures in the law made permanent.

Losing Freedoms and Democracy Section by Section

Under the Patriot Act, it is legal for the government to:

— **Look at your private medical records, what you buy, what you study and what books you read.** Section 215 of the Patriot Act gives the FBI and other law enforcement agencies access to a broad variety of personal records without having to have probable cause or obtain a search warrant. It also makes it a crime for those who are compelled to turn over records—be they business owners, doctors, librarians, etc.—to reveal that they have been forced to give up the information.

— **Search your home without telling you.** Under Section 213, the government can conduct secret "sneak and peek" searches of an individual's home or office. They can take pictures, seize property and even collect DNA samples—without ever having to tell the individual that a warrant was issued.

— **Label protesters who engage in civil disobedience as "domestic terrorists."** Under Section 802 of the Patriot Act, "domestic terrorism" is defined as any act that is "dangerous to human life," involves a violation of any state or federal law, and is intended to influence government policy. That definition is so broad that it could apply to protesters at an antiwar march where there are minor acts of vandalism, or a civil disobedience action where protesters resist arrest.

— **Seize business and financial records.** Section 505 allows the government to use National Security Letters (NSLs) to seize business and financial records—as well as, in some instances, the membership lists of organizations that provide Internet service. In November [2006], the *Washington Post* revealed that the FBI now issues more than 30,000 National Security Letters each year—up from a few hundred a year before the Patriot Act.

— **Detain immigrants for a week without charges—and indefinitely on minor charges.** Section 412 allows the attorney general to "certify" that an immigrant or non-citizen is a terrorist or a threat to national security—without having to show probable cause or charge or convict them of any specific crime. That person can then be detained for a week without being charged with any crime. They can be detained longer, as long as the government can find an excuse like a minor immigration violation to charge them with. And if a suspect in jail on an immigration violation cannot be deported, they can be detained indefinitely—as long as the attorney general certifies every six months that national security is at stake.

An Innocent Victim of the War on Terror

The Bush administration insists that all this is protecting Americans. Bush recently told reporters that, in passing the Patriot Act in 2001, "Members from both parties came together and said we will give those on the front line of

protecting America the tools necessary to protect American citizens, and at the same time, guard the civil liberties of our citizens."

But most of those charged under the Patriot Act have no ties to terrorism. And ask Portland, Ore., lawyer and practicing Muslim Brandon Mayfield if he feels like his civil liberties were "guarded."

In 2004, Mayfield was arrested as a material witness in connection with the March 2004 bombings in Madrid, Spain, that killed 191 people. The government used Section 218 of the Patriot Act to carry out a secret search of Mayfield's home without a warrant. The FBI entered Mayfield's home and copied four computer drives, digitally photographed documents, seized 10 DNA samples and took approximately 335 digital photographs.

But Brandon Mayfield was completely innocent—and spent more than two weeks in jail before the FBI finally figured out he was misidentified.

Incredibly, a report issued by the Justice Department earlier this month [January 2006] claims that Mayfield's arrest, the invasion of his home and the smearing of his name had nothing to do with the government's use of the Patriot Act—but rather with "overconfidence" in finger-printing techniques.

Seventeen Months in Jail

Brandon Mayfield isn't the only innocent victim.

In 2004, Muslim intellectual Tariq Ramadan had his visa to teach at the University of Notre Dame revoked under Section 411 of the Patriot Act, which allows the government to bar anyone from the country who has or will use a "position of prominence . . . to endorse or espouse terrorist activity." Ramadan has condemned terrorism, but because he is an outspoken critic of the Israeli government's war on Palestinians—and the U.S. policies that support it—that was enough to get him barred from the U.S.

In 2003, Sami al-Hussayen, a student at the University of Idaho, was arrested and prosecuted under Section 805 of the Patriot Act, which makes it a crime to lend "expert advice and assistance" to a terrorist organization. His crime? While working as the Internet administrator for the Islamic Assembly of North America, he listed links on the site to speeches by prominent Muslim scholars—including some that allegedly advocated criminal activity and suicide operations.

A former CIA official testifying on behalf of al-Hussayen said the sites linked to the student appeared to be analytical and religious in nature, not terrorist tools—and after an eight week trial, a jury found al-Hussayen not guilty on terrorism charges. But the Feds continued to pursue immigration charges against the student. In all, al-Hussayen spent 17 months in an Idaho jail, before finally agreeing to "voluntary" deportation. . . .

The War on Democracy

Patriot Act 2 is fundamentally flawed because it relies on a false premise—that America can be safer if we do away with basic checks and balances. By undermining the role of the courts, Congress and the press in providing a real check on executive power, Patriot Act 2 directs its ire at the institutions of our democracy instead of at the terrorists that threaten it. In so doing, it threatens to undermine the rights of ordinary people and, ironically, the war against terrorism.

American Civil Liberties Union, "Fact Sheet on PATRIOT Act II," March 28, 2003. http://www.aclu.org/safefree/general/17383leg20030328.html.

The Racism of the War on Terror

While the Patriot Act is an attack on all of our rights, Arabs and Muslims have borne the brunt of the abuses committed in the name of "fighting terrorism."

A 2003 Justice Department report into the treatment of detainees found systematic abuse carried out by as many as 20 guards at a Brooklyn detention center. Among the problems detailed were "unnecessary and inappropriate use of strip searches and banging on detainees' cell doors excessively while they were trying to sleep."

"We did not find evidence that the detainees were brutally beaten, but we found evidence some officers slammed and bounced detainees against the wall, twisted their arms and hands in painful ways, stepped on their leg restraint chains and punished them by keeping them restrained for long periods of time," the report said.

As *Socialist Worker* went to press, six detainees—all of whom spent weeks or months in jail and were eventually cleared of any connection to terrorism before being deported anyway—were returning temporarily to the U.S. to begin depositions in a lawsuit brought against government officials, including former Attorney General John Ashcroft and FBI Director Robert Mueller.

Government officials like U.S. attorney Jim Letten have spoken in favor of the USA PATRIOT Act as important to protecting Americans from terrorists.

No Right to Sue

Despite the government's own report detailing abuses inside the detention center, the Justice Department refuses to admit any wrongdoing, claiming that September 11 attacks created "special factors" that override detainees' right to sue for damages for any constitutional violation.

But as Center for Constitutional Rights (CCR) lawyer Rachel Meeropol, who represents two of the former detainees, told the *New York Times*, "The post-9/11 domestic immigration sweeps were the first example of the Bush administration's willingness to ignore the law and hold people outside the judicial system. The kind of torture, interrogation and arbitrary detention that we now associate with Guantánamo and secret CIA facilities really started right here, in Brooklyn."

The Right to Assemble Is In Jeopardy

Protesting against the Bush administration could become a lot more difficult if the latest version of the Patriot Act passes without revision.

Currently, the Secret Service is authorized to charge suspects with breaching security or disruptive behavior at National Special Security Events—but only if the president or another person under the protection of the service is in attendance.

Last month, it was revealed that under the latest version of the Act, protesters could be tossed into jail for even less. The new bill would allow the Secret Service to cordon off areas, enforce exclusion zones and jail people for disruptive behavior at any event deemed a "special event of national significance," even if no one under Secret Service protection were scheduled to speak or attend.

Judging from news reports, the Secret Service's definition of "disruptive behavior" includes anyone expressing an opinion contrary to the president's.

Arrested for Political T-Shirts—What's Next?

In 2004, for example, Nicole and Jeff Rank were arrested by the Secret Service in Charleston, W. Va.—for wearing T-shirts that read "Love America, Hate Bush" and "Regime change starts at home" to the president's July 4 appearance. Last March, the Secret Service expelled two Denver students from a "town hall" forum on Social Security reform with President Bush—because they had an anti-war bumper sticker on their car.

If the new provision is passed, people like these could be arrested at any "special events of national significance," which, according to the *Washington Post*, could include everything from political conventions to the Olympics.

Analyze the essay:

1. Colson relates the story of Brandon Mayfield as an example of how the war on terror threatens freedom and democracy. Explain Mayfield's predicament. Then explain whether you consider his case to be a sign that democracy and freedom are under threat. Use evidence from the text to support your answer.

2. Colson believes the provisions contained in the Patriot Act pose severe threats to American democracy. What do you think? Are the measures Colson describes violations of rights and liberties? Or will they help catch terrorists who may be living in America? Explain your view of the Patriot Act and to what extent freedom and democracy should be curtailed to ensure safety.

American Democracy Is Not Threatened by the War on Terror

Daniel Krauthammer

In the following essay author Daniel Krauthammer argues that American democracy is not threatened by the war on terror. He discusses the National Security Agency's domestic wiretapping program, which was secretly authorized by President George W. Bush in 2002. The program allows federal authorities to listen in on the American public's conversations without first obtaining a warrant. Krauthammer argues that such surveillance is legal under the Authorization for Use of Military Force (AUMF) provision that was passed after September 11. AUMF granted the president the authority to use all necessary force to catch terrorists—and Krauthammer maintains that warrantless wiretapping is part and parcel of that effort. He argues that issuing warrants wastes time and alerts would-be terrorists to the fact that authorities are onto them. For all of these reasons, Krauthammer concludes that warrantless surveillance programs in the war on terror are legal and necessary, and as such do not conflict with American freedom and democracy.

Krauthammer graduated from Harvard University in 2007. His articles have appeared in the *Harvard Political Review*, one of America's most prestigious undergraduate journals of politics and public policy. He is the son of conservative columnist Charles Krauthammer.

Daniel Krauthammer, "Bush's Wiretapping: Legal and Necessary," *Harvard Political Review*, March 18, 2006. Reproduced by permission.

Consider the following questions:

1. What does Krauthammer call the NSA wire-tapping program a prime example of?
2. Why is domestic warrantless wiretapping not a violation of the Fourth Amendment, in Krauthammer's opinion?
3. What is the Foreign Intelligence Surveillance Act (FISA), and why does the author believe it cannot constitutionally forbid warrantless searches?

In the days after September 11 [2001], a myriad of polls showed that the American people believed more catastrophic terrorist attacks were on their way. It has been more than four years now, and the United States hasn't suffered a single terrorist strike on its soil. This blessed fact is certainly not due to a change of heart on Al Qaeda's part. It is due to the implementation of a vast array of new counterterrorist strategies and policies on the part of this government. The recently revealed, secret NSA [National Security Agency] wiretapping program is an important piece of this broad strategy, and the great barrage of criticism that has been aimed against it is misguided. The program is a prime example of the kind of counterterrorist measures that are both absolutely necessary in the War on Terror and also perfectly legal.

Wiretapping Does Not Threaten American Democracy or Freedom

A careful examination of relevant legislation and precedent shows that the law clearly allows the NSA's use of unwarranted wiretaps on international communications between persons in the United States and suspected terrorists abroad. To begin, the program operates comfortably within the bounds of the Constitution and does not, as some mistakenly believe, violate the Fourth Amendment. Warrants are required for domestic search and seizure, but in decision such as *Katz v. United States* and *United States v. United States District Court*,[1] the Supreme Court specifically allowed an exception to the warrant requirement for domestic surveillance conducted for foreign intelligence purposes.

The Threat Is from Terrorists, Not from Law Enforcement

The fundamental question facing Americans today is not the false tradeoff between security and liberty, but rather how we can use security to protect liberty. Any debate over security and liberty must start with the recognition that the primary threat to American freedom comes from al-Qaeda and other groups that seek to kill Americans, not from the men and women of law enforcement agencies who protect them from that danger.

Viet D. Dinh, "How the USA Patriot Act Defends Democracy," Foundation for the Defense of Democracies, June 1, 2004. http://www.defend democracy. org/usr_doc/USA_Patriot_Act_2.pdf.

The Lack of Warrants Is Perfectly Constitutional

The only real argument against the legality of the wiretapping program is that the Foreign Intelligence Surveillance Act (FISA) requires that, for this kind of domestic surveillance, the NSA present evidence and obtain a warrant from a secret FISA court. There are two reasons this law is not binding for the current NSA program. First, FISA specifically allows for exception to its requirements when "authorized by statute," and the Authorization for Use of Military Force (AUMF), passed by Congress after September 11, constitutes just such a statute. It authorizes the president "to use all necessary and appropriate force against those nations, organizations, or persons he determines planned, authorized, committed, or aided the terrorist attacks that occurred on September 11, 2001, or harbored such organizations or persons." The act gave the president extraordinary powers to fight Al Qaeda— powers that made clear exception to normal rules. In *Hamdi v. Rumsfeld*,[2] the Supreme Court interpreted AUMF as "an Act of Congress" that, as with the FISA "statue," made excep-

1. A 1967 case in which the U.S. Supreme Court ruled on the requirements of the Fourth Amendment in cases of domestic surveillance.

2. The 2004 court case in which the Supreme Court recognized the power of the government to detain unlawful combatants.

Sinn Fein president Gerry Adams holds a wiretapping device. Wiretapping devices may become more commonplace in America because surveillance equipment is legal under the Authorization for Use of Military Force (AUMF) provision, which was passed after the September 11th terrorist attacks.

tion to a law prohibiting the detention of persons without trial. If AUMF can provide a legal basis to deny trial to a U.S. citizen in detention, then certainly it must allow for a comparatively mild wiretap.

Second, even were the AUMF exception to be discounted, it is extremely questionable whether FISA itself is constitutional. The act is essentially an attempt by Congress to reign in presidential power, but it is an unjustifiable

Most Americans Approve of War on Terror Tactics

A 2006 *Washington Post*–ABC News Poll found the following about American attitudes about democracy and freedom in the context of the war on terror:

Question: What do you think is more important right now—for the federal government to investigate possible terrorist threats, even if that intrudes on personal privacy; or for the federal government not to intrude on personal privacy, even if that limits its ability to invesitgate possible terrorist threats?

No Opinion **4%**

Respect Privacy **31%** **65%** Investigate Threats

Question: It's been reported that the National Security Agency has been collecting the phone call records of tens of millions of Americans. It then analyzes calling patterns in an effort to identify possible terrorism suspects, without listening to or recording the conversations. Would you consider this an acceptable or unacceptable way for the federal government to invesitigate terrorism?

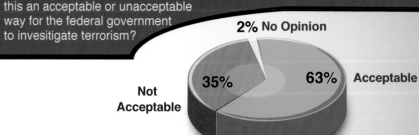

2% No Opinion

Not Acceptable **35%** **63%** Acceptable

Question: If you found out that the NSA had a record of phone numbers that you yourself have called, would that bother you, or not?

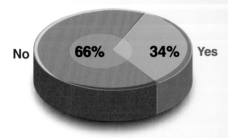

No **66%** **34%** Yes

Taken from: "*Washington Post*—ABC News Poll," *Washington Post*, May 12, 2006.
http://www.washingtonpost.com/wp-srv/politics/polls/postpoll_nsa_051206.htm.

attempt, as it is solely to the executive branch that the Constitution grants authority over all matters concerning the conduct of war and protection of national security. Indeed, since FISA was passed in 1978, no president, Democrat or Republican, has acknowledged its constitutionality or its right to limit presidential power. President [Bill] Clinton's deputy attorney general stated the standard view from all administrations when she testified that "the Department of Justice believes, and the case law supports, that the president has inherent authority to conduct warrantless physical searches for foreign intelligence purposes." The courts have upheld this position as well. A November 2002 decision of the FISA Court of Review stated that "the President did have inherent authority to conduct warrantless searches to obtain foreign intelligence information. . . . We take for granted that the President does

By working with world leaders (such as Afghanistan's President Hamid Karzai, left), President Bush hopes to keep the United States safe from another terrorist attack.

have that authority and, assuming that is so, FISA could not encroach on the President's constitutional power."

Legal and Necessary

President Bush's NSA wiretapping program is thus clearly legal. And it is very necessary. At the end of the day, it's important that our intelligence services be listening in when someone in America is making an international call to a friend in Al Qaeda. Were the NSA required to obtain warrants for such eavesdropping, valuable information gathering could be delayed and access denied to the communications of suspected but unproven terrorists. It is often said that we didn't connect the dots before September 11. Let's not let it happen again.

Analyze the essay:

1. Krauthammer concludes his essay by reminding readers that on September 11, 2001, authorities "failed to connect the dots." Do you think this was an effective way to drive home his argument? Why or why not?

2. Krauthammer and Colson (author of the previous viewpoint) disagree on whether the war on terror compromises American freedom and democracy. After reading both essays, with which author do you agree? What ideas or pieces of evidence convinced you? Cite them in your answer.

The United States Should Bring Democracy to Other Countries

George W. Bush

George W. Bush is the forty-third president of the United States. The following speech was delivered when he was sworn into his second term in office in 2005. In it Bush explains why he believes America should spread democracy around the world. Bush claims that democracy must be spread to ensure America's own safety: When people live under tyranny, he says, they are exposed to violence, instability, and anger, which are all key causes of terrorism. To reduce terrorism and increase peace around the world, therefore, Bush recommends that democracy and freedom be supported in all nations. Since its founding America has believed in the freedom of every individual, and Bush encourages Americans to support freedom and democracy not just at home, but abroad. He promises America's support to those around the world who are unjustly jailed or denied the right to vote. Bush concludes that the best way to preserve American democracy is to support the birth of democratic institutions and movements around the globe.

Consider the following questions:
1. What will America refuse to pretend, according to Bush?
2. Bush opens his speech by recalling a "day of fire"—to what event is he referring?
3. What does the phrase "task of arms" mean in the context of the essay?

George W. Bush, "President Sworn in to Second Term," in www.whitehouse.gov, January 20, 2005.

On this day, prescribed by law and marked by ceremony, we celebrate the durable wisdom of our Constitution, and recall the deep commitments that unite our country. I am grateful for the honor of this hour, mindful of the consequential times in which we live, and determined to fulfill the oath that I have sworn and you have witnessed.

At this . . . gathering, our duties are defined not by the words I use, but by the history we have seen together. For a half century, America defended our own freedom by standing watch on distant borders. After the shipwreck of communism came years of relative quiet, years of repose, years of sabbatical—and then there came a day of fire.

The Force of Human Freedom

We have seen our vulnerability—and we have seen its deepest source. For as long as whole regions of the world simmer in resentment and tyranny—prone to ideologies that feed hatred and excuse murder—violence will gather, and multiply in destructive power, and cross the most defended borders, and raise a mortal threat. There is only one force of history that can break the reign of hatred and resentment, and expose the pretensions of tyrants, and reward the hopes of the decent and tolerant, and that is the force of human freedom.

We are led, by events and common sense, to one conclusion: The survival of liberty in our land increasingly depends on the success of liberty in other lands. The best hope for peace in our world is the expansion of freedom in all the world.

America's Policy Must Be to Spread Democracy

America's vital interests and our deepest beliefs are now one. From the day of our Founding, we have proclaimed that every man and woman on this earth has rights, and dignity, and matchless value, because they bear the image of the Maker of Heaven and earth. Across the generations we have proclaimed the imperative of self-government, because no one is fit to be a master, and no one deserves to be a slave. Advancing these ideals is the mission that created our Nation. It is the honorable achievement of our fathers. Now it is the urgent requirement of our nation's security, and the calling of our time.

So it is the policy of the United States to seek and support the growth of democratic movements and institutions in every nation and culture, with the ultimate goal of ending tyranny in our world.

This is not primarily the task of arms, though we will defend ourselves and our friends by force of arms when necessary. Freedom, by its nature, must be chosen, and defended by citizens, and sustained by the rule of law and the protection of minorities. And when the soul of a nation finally speaks, the institutions that arise may reflect customs and traditions very different from our own. America will not impose our own style of government on the unwilling. Our

The United States Capitol building has become a symbol for freedom and democracy in the United States, and Americans hope to export such values around the world.

Democracy, Government, and Liberty Around the World

In 2006 the *Economist* undertook a substantial project to rank the world's fully democratic countries by their government, political participation, political culture, and civil liberties.

Full Democracies	Rank	Overall Score	Functioning of Government	Political Participation	Political Culture	Civil Liberties
Sweden	1	9.88	10.00	10.00	9.38	10.00
Iceland	2	9.71	9.64	8.89	10.00	10.00
Netherlands	3	9.66	9.29	9.44	10.00	10.00
Norway	4	9.55	9.64	10.00	8.13	10.00
Denmark	5	9.52	9.64	8.89	9.38	9.71
Finland	6	9.25	10.00	7.78	8.75	9.71
Luxembourg	7	9.10	9.29	7.78	8.75	9.71
Australia	8	9.09	8.93	7.78	8.75	10.00
Canada	9	9.07	9.64	7.78	8.75	10.00
Switzerland	10	9.02	9.29	7.78	8.75	9.71
Ireland	11	9.01	8.93	7.78	8.75	10.00
New Zealand	12	9.01	8.57	8.33	8.13	10.00
Germany	13	8.82	8.57	7.78	8.75	9.41
Austria	14	8.69	8.21	7.78	8.75	9.12
Malta	15	8.39	8.21	6.11	8.75	9.71
Spain	16	8.34	7.86	6.11	8.75	9.41
United States	17	8.22	7.86	7.22	8.75	8.53
Czech Republic	18	8.17	6.79	7.22	8.13	9.12
Portugal	19	8.16	8.21	6.11	7.50	9.41
Belgium	20	8.15	8.21	6.67	6.88	9.41
Japan	20	8.15	7.86	5.56	8.75	9.41
Greece	22	8.13	7.50	6.67	7.50	9.41
United Kingdom	23	8.08	8.57	5.00	8.13	9.12
France	24	8.07	7.50	6.67	7.50	9.12
Mauritius	25	8.04	8.21	5.00	8.13	9.71
Costa Rica	25	8.04	8.21	6.11	6.88	9.41
Slovenia	27	7.96	7.86	6.67	6.88	8.82
Uruguay	27	7.96	8.21	5.00	6.88	9.71

Taken from: The *Economist*.

goal instead is to help others find their own voice, attain their own freedom, and make their own way.

The great objective of ending tyranny is the concentrated work of generations. The difficulty of the task is no excuse for avoiding it. America's influence is not unlimited, but fortunately for the oppressed, America's influence is considerable, and we will use it confidently in freedom's cause.

Oppression Is Always Wrong, Freedom Always Right

My most solemn duty is to protect this nation and its people against further attacks and emerging threats. Some have unwisely chosen to test America's resolve, and have found it firm.

We will persistently clarify the choice before every ruler and every nation: The moral choice between oppression, which is always wrong, and freedom, which is eternally right. America will not pretend that jailed dissidents prefer their chains, or that women welcome humiliation and servitude, or that any human being aspires to live at the mercy of bullies.

We will encourage reform in other governments by making clear that success in our relations will require the decent treatment of their own people. America's belief in human dignity will guide our policies, yet rights must be more than the grudging concessions of dictators; they are secured by free dissent and the participation of the governed. In the long run, there is no justice without freedom, and there can be no human rights without human liberty.

Some, I know, have questioned the global appeal of liberty—though this time in history, four decades defined by the swiftest advance of freedom ever seen, is an odd

> ## Democracy Provides an Alternative for Tomorrow's Terrorists
>
> To win the war on terror, America must defeat today's terrorists and prevent the recruitment of tomorrow's. One of the best ways to prevent recruitment is to make clear that life holds real opportunity. Young people in the Arab world as elsewhere yearn for the freedom to be heard, to stand for something larger than self, to control their own destinies and to choose their own leaders. Only democracy can fulfill these aspirations.
>
> Liz Cheney, "Why America Must Promote Democracy in the Middle East," ABC News, September 17, 2007. http://abcnews.go.com/Politics/Story?id=3611675&page=1.

time for doubt. Americans, of all people, should never be surprised by the power of our ideals. Eventually, the call of freedom comes to every mind and every soul. We do not accept the existence of permanent tyranny because we do not accept the possibility of permanent slavery. Liberty will come to those who love it.

Promoting Democracy Helps Defeat Our Enemies

Today, America speaks anew to the peoples of the world:

All who live in tyranny and hopelessness can know: the United States will not ignore your oppression, or excuse your oppressors. When you stand for your liberty, we will stand with you.

Democratic reformers facing repression, prison, or exile can know: America sees you for who you are: the future leaders of your free country.

The rulers of outlaw regimes can know that we still believe as Abraham Lincoln did: "Those who deny freedom to others deserve it not for themselves; and, under the rule of a just God, cannot long retain it."

The leaders of governments with long habits of control need to know: To serve your people you must learn to trust them. Start on this journey of progress and justice, and America will walk at your side.

And all the allies of the United States can know: we honor your friendship, we rely on your counsel, and we depend on your help. Division among free nations is a primary goal of freedom's enemies. The concerted effort of free nations to promote democracy is a prelude to our enemies' defeat. . . .

Democracy: The Goal of Our Generation

From the perspective of a single day, including this day of dedication, the issues and questions before our country are many. From the viewpoint of centuries, the questions that come to us are narrowed and few. Did our generation advance the cause of freedom? And did our character bring credit to that cause?

These questions that judge us also unite us, because Americans of every party and background, Americans by choice and by birth, are bound to one another in the cause of freedom. We have known divisions, which must be healed to move forward in great purposes—and I will strive in good faith to heal them. Yet those divisions do not define America. We felt the unity and fellowship of our nation when freedom came under attack, and our response came like a single hand over a single heart. And we can feel that same unity and pride whenever America acts for good, and the victims of disaster are given hope, and the unjust encounter justice, and the captives are set free.

Freedom and Democracy Will Triumph

We go forward with complete confidence in the eventual triumph of freedom. Not because history runs on the

U.S. Secretary of State Condoleezza Rice meets with foreign ministers from Spain and Britain to discuss plans to spread democracy in the Middle East.

wheels of inevitability; it is human choices that move events. Not because we consider ourselves a chosen nation; God moves and chooses as He wills. We have confidence because freedom is the permanent hope of mankind, the hunger in dark places, the longing of the soul. When our Founders declared a new order of the ages; when soldiers died in wave upon wave for a union based on liberty; when citizens marched in peaceful outrage under the banner "Freedom Now"—they were acting on an ancient hope that is meant to be fulfilled. History has an ebb and flow of justice, but history also has a visible direction, set by liberty and the Author of Liberty.

When the Declaration of Independence was first read in public and the Liberty Bell was sounded in celebration, a witness said, "It rang as if it meant something." In our time it means something still. America, in this young century, proclaims liberty throughout all the world, and to all the inhabitants thereof. Renewed in our strength—tested, but not weary—we are ready for the greatest achievements in the history of freedom.

Analyze the essay:

1. Bush claims that spreading democracy to nations around the world will result in world peace and stability. How do you think John F. McManus, author of the following essay, would respond to that claim?

2. Bush appeals to his listeners' sense of emotion in order to persuade them to agree with his point. To this end he invokes their history, sense of patriotism, and the horrors of the September 11 terrorist attacks. How did these appeals to emotion color your reception of his argument? Did they make you more or less likely to agree with him? Explain your answer using evidence from the text.

The United States Should Not Bring Democracy to Other Countries

John F. McManus

In the following essay author John F. McManus explains why the United States should not attempt to impose democracy on other countries. For one, says McManus, when democracy is imposed on countries that are not ready for it, the resulting system is often superficial, unstable, or false. He cites U.S. efforts to bring democracy to Afghanistan and Iraq as evidence that democracy cannot simply be dropped and embraced by nations with complicated cultural, religious, and geopolitical histories. Secondly McManus reminds readers that democracy is at heart the ability of the majority of people to choose their own government. While that sounds well and good, McManus argues that many times the majority of people will democratically elect an undemocratic government. This occurred in the Palestinian Territories in 2006 when Palestinians democratically elected the terrorist group Hamas into power. For these reasons McManus warns leaders against assuming that efforts to spread democracy will benefit the United States.

McManus is president of the John Birch Society, a Wisconsin-based organization that is committed to personal freedom, limited government, and preserving freedom under the U.S. Constitution. The Society publishes the *New American,* where this essay was originally published.

John F. McManus, "Democracy Isn't the Answer," *The New American*, vol. 22, May 1, 2006, p. 44. Copyright © 2006 American Opinion Publishing Incorporated. Reproduced by permission.

The justification for the war in Iraq has morphed over time. At first it was the dangers of weapons of mass destruction (WMD), then it became a fight against terrorism. And then even terrorism in general proved to be an elusive justification for the war and its mounting casualties. The attacks against U.S. forces in Iraq have continued mainly because the Americans are looked upon as interlopers by the people placing their bombs along roadsides. They are retaliating against foreign meddling in their nation's affairs. They clearly resent the United States imposing our nation's will on them.

So, having gone from WMD threats to terrorism, the justification for the American action in Iraq has become the need to build "democracy." And democracy, according to this administration, will be achieved when people choose their own form of government and their own leaders. But what if the people decide on something harmful to themselves and dangerous to mankind? What if long-standing divisions among the people—such as religious factionalism in Iraq—result in civil war? In other words, what if democracy isn't the answer?

American Attempts to Spread Democracy Are Often Superficial or False

Last October [2005], Secretary of State Condoleezza Rice trekked all the way to Afghanistan where she expressed great delight because the nation was "now inspiring the world with its march toward democracy." The cause of her joy? Afghans had conducted an election and selected a president along with an elected parliament. But warlords still control much of the country; a high percentage of the nation's international trade is in heroin; and the reigning Islamic clerics remain determined to execute anyone who abandons the Muslim faith for some other belief. Isn't democracy wonderful!

In his most recent State of the Union address, President Bush gushed about "the dramatic progress of a new democracy" in Iraq. Yes, the Iraqi people voted to choose

Democracy does not necessarily guarantee the election of just government leaders. For example, in 2006, Palestinians elected the terrorist group Hamas into power.

Americans Support Promoting Democracy, but in Limited Forms

A 2005 World Public Opinion study found that Americans support the promotion of democracy, but only by a few methods. The majority of Americans do not support spreading democracy if it means withholding aid, using military force, or supporting dissidents.

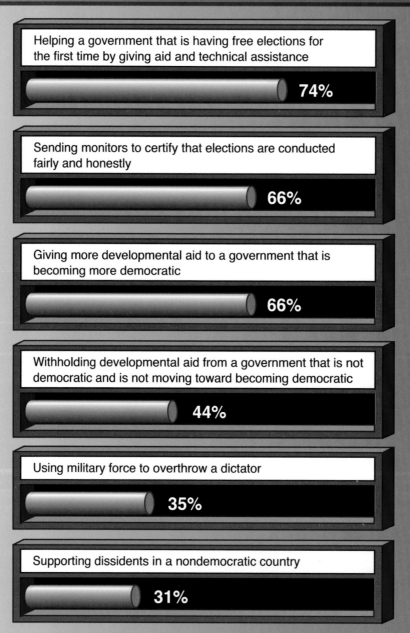

Helping a government that is having free elections for the first time by giving aid and technical assistance

74%

Sending monitors to certify that elections are conducted fairly and honestly

66%

Giving more developmental aid to a government that is becoming more democratic

66%

Withholding developmental aid from a government that is not democratic and is not moving toward becoming democratic

44%

Using military force to overthrow a dictator

35%

Supporting dissidents in a nondemocratic country

31%

Source: "U.S. Role in the World: Promoting Democracy and Human Rights," World Public Opinion.org. www.americans-world.org/digest/overview/us_role/democracy.cfm.

a new government with a new leader under a new constitution. But, in the absence of a strong government that could control internecine animosities, the Shiites began warring with the Sunnis, and the Kurds remain waiting in the wings to take control when the other two factions exhaust themselves. Also, Shiites and Sunnis each harbor resentment because the United States is looked upon as favoring their adversary. So American military personnel are still getting picked off two, three, or ten at a time. Isn't it a bit absurd to be lauding democracy in Iraq?

Democracy Is an Invitation to Chaos

Democracy, as America's Founding Fathers well knew, is an invitation to chaos and eventual tyranny. The men who created this nation knew the results of the democracies in the pre-Christian Greek city states, and they were horrified at what democracy had produced. But these same men also studied the success that marked ancient Rome where a written constitution limited the power of government.

The key to success in Rome was recognition of the inherent rights of man and limitation of government to a role that saw it empowered only to protect rights. Did a majority of the people have power to promote its faction? Absolutely not. There has to be restraint on the powerful. History shows that expecting restraint to come from a majority of the people (the essence of democracy) is expecting the impossible.

It Is Not Fair for the U.S. to Spread Democracy

There is a passionate resistance to the U.S. "imposing" its style of democracy to suit American purposes. Democratic reformers in the Middle East don't want to have their own hopes and dreams subordinated to the political agenda of the United States. It's for this reason that ... democracy can't be imposed—it has to be homegrown.

Wesley Clark, "War Didn't and Doesn't Bring Democracy," *Washington Monthly*, May 2005.

Democratic Movements Have Resulted in Undemocratic Regimes

Nowadays, over in Israel, the Palestinians were given a chance to vote for leaders, and the people chose the terrorists in Hamas. Democracy triumphed!

In Venezuela, the people chose Hugo Chavez, an outright Marxist and a determined enemy of our nation. Using his country's oil wealth, he's hard at work spreading Marxism throughout Latin America. Similarity, the peoples of Brazil, Chile, and elsewhere in South America have voted outright Marxist dictators into office. The future will find them regretting what they have done. Let's hope they will eventually understand that democracy isn't the answer.

Democracy Does Not Always Lead to Stability and Peace

At the end of World War II, the leaders of some war-torn nations looked to the United States for guidelines about how to reconstruct their governments. If they went to the right sources, they were urged to build a constitutionally limited government whose powers were directed almost exclusively toward protecting the life, liberty, and property of every citizen. Under such a system, there would be no factions grasping for power, no demagogues appealing for votes, and no sliding into totalitarianism. But if they went to the wrong sources, as many did, they were encouraged to turn to democracy where the voice of the people—no matter what it chooses—is considered the ultimate seat of wisdom.

In 1928, the U.S. government published Training Manual 2000–05 to teach members of the armed forces about citizenship. The manual described democracy as a "government of the masses" that should be rejected. It further stated: "Attitude toward law is that the will of the majority shall regulate. . . . Results in demagogism, license, agitation, discontent, anarchy."

Those were the days when many Americans knew what democracy really meant, and when they knew that our nation was founded as a republic. A return to understanding the wonders of a constitutional republic and the horrors of a democracy is long overdue.

Analyze the essay:

1. McManus uses the examples of the Palestinian Territories and Venezuela to show that governments chosen by the majority—or democratically—may not end up being democratic at all. In the case of the Palestinian Territories, Palestinians elected representatives from Hamas, a known terrorist group. What problems does this pose for the United States? In your opinion, should the United States support the Palestinians' choice of Hamas, or not? Explain your reasoning.

2. McManus uses sarcasm to get some of his points across. Where does he use this technique? In your opinion, does it strengthen or weaken his essay?

Spreading Democracy Will Reduce Terrorism

Douglas J. Feith

In the following essay author Douglas J. Feith argues that spreading democracy is the best way to eradicate terrorism. He likens the current war on terrorism to the struggle against communism during the Cold War, arguing that just as the promotion of freedom and democracy helped defeat communism, so will it help defeat terrorism. He says that the war on terror cannot be won if the United States merely attacks terrorist networks. Because terrorists rely on anger, oppression, and injustice to rally people to their cause, Feith believes the United States must change the unjust conditions that breed terrorism and replace them with democracy and freedom. He says particular attention should be paid to spreading democracy in the Middle East because that region is a source of both oppression and terrorism. Finally Feith discusses Iraq as a place in which the battle of ideas between democracy and terrorism is being waged. He concludes it is vital for the safety and freedom of people everywhere that America wins this battle and that democracy prevails.

Feith was the undersecretary of defense for policy in the Bush administration from 2001–2005. He has held several high-ranking government positions, including Middle East specialist on the National Security Council (NSC) under President Ronald Reagan in 1981.

Consider the following questions:

1. Who is Edmund Burke, and how does he factor into Feith's argument?
2. What does Feith mean when he says that terrorism must become like the slave trade?
3. What will the Middle East remain a place of if freedom does not flourish there, according to Feith?

Douglas J. Feith, "Defense, Democracy and the War on Terrorism," in U.S. Department of Defense Speeches, April 23, 2004.

As many of us in the Reagan Administration saw it, the Cold War was fundamentally about protecting the freedom—the lives and civil liberties—of the United States and our allies.

We won the Cold War while avoiding World War III, a rather amazing strategic accomplishment for which the world is a better place. But we find that our lives and civil liberties—our security and freedom—are threatened seriously again—now from other quarters—in particular from al Qaida and its network of fellow terrorist groups and their state and non-state supporters.

As promoting freedom for others was a potent element of our strategy for winning the Cold War, so it serves as

German citizens celebrate the end of communism in East Germany by tearing down the Berlin Wall. The historic occasion represented the triumph of freedom and democracy in that region.

an important element in our strategy for winning the war on terrorism today.

How to Spread Democracy

Some assume that when US policymakers discuss promoting freedom we mean creating systems of government in other countries that look like the American Constitutional system. But that isn't the case.

The 18th century British political philosopher Edmund Burke gives us some useful guidance in thinking about the championing abroad of freedom and democratic political institutions. Burke wrote at a time when the fervor of the French Revolution was sending tremors through Europe. Burke cautioned against enthusiasm for theory—against the dangers to liberty and human happiness that can arise from political abstractions. He warned that successful political institutions are rooted in tradition and rely on organic connections to the local soil and culture.

These are weighty admonitions. They tell us to respect the importance of the differences between societies long accustomed to democratic practices and other societies. And they highlight for us the magnitude of the task of encouraging democratic development in the latter societies.

Burke's admonitions, however, do not mean that countries without experience of democratic government are doomed forever to remain undemocratic. There are too many examples from the last half-century of successful new democracies in Asia, Latin America and Europe for us to believe that.

> ## Lack of Democracy Is a Key Cause of Terror
>
> More terrorists do come from poor countries than rich ones, but this is because poor countries tend to lack civil liberties. . . . Countries like Saudi Arabia and Bahrain, which have spawned relatively many terrorists, are economically well off yet lacking in civil liberties. Poor countries with a tradition of protecting civil liberties are unlikely to spawn terrorists. Evidently, the freedom to assemble and protest peacefully without interference from the government goes a long way to providing an alternative to terrorism.
>
> Alan B. Krueger, "Cash Rewards and Poverty Alone Do Not Explain Terrorism," *New York Times*, May 29, 2003, p. C2.

Spreading Democracy Is Strategic

Successive US administrations have promoted freedom abroad for a variety of good reasons. Among the princi-

The Connection Between Terrorism and Oppression

The world's least-free countries–such as Saudi Arabia, Syria, and Pakistan–have ongoing problems with terrorism.

Free   Partly free   Not free

Taken from: Freedom House, 2006.

pal good reasons for our doing so now is the role that democratic institution-building can play in our strategy for the war on terrorism.

We cannot win this war if all we do is disrupt and attack terrorist networks. Terrorist groups can recruit and indoctrinate new terrorists faster and far more inexpensively than the US and its coalition partners can capture or kill them.

Victory for the coalition will require us to counter ideological support for terrorism—to reduce the flow of new recruits into the terrorists' ranks. This task has at least two parts: First, the de-legitimation of terrorism, making terrorism (as President Bush has put) like the slave trade, piracy on the high seas and genocide, activities that no respectable person can condone, much less support.

The second part is support for models of political and philosophical moderation, especially in the Muslim world. Championing freedom can make a contribution here.

Democracy and the War on Terror: "Inextricably Linked"

As the distinguished scholar of Islam, Professor Bernard Lewis, put it: "The war against terror and the quest for freedom are inextricably linked—neither can succeed without the other."

That's why President Bush outlined what he calls a "forward strategy for freedom in the Middle East." As he puts it, so long as freedom does not flourish, the Middle East "will remain a place of stagnation, resentment and violence ready for export."

President Bush does not have the view that a particular governmental structure suits every person and every society. But he does believe that the aspiration for freedom is inherent in people everywhere. The societies that best satisfy that hope are those that enjoy the greatest stability, creativity and prosperity.

President Bush often speaks of the sources of the liberal impulse—the God-given desire for personal freedom. But he does not believe in "one size fits all" or "cookie cutter" answers to the complex questions facing developing countries. President Bush, if I can put it this way, champions freedom without violating the precepts of Edmund Burke.

Democratic Societies Tend to Flourish

We know from experience that some of the world's more grievous ills can be solved or mitigated by giving people governments that allow them to live freely. The good effects reach far beyond politics. Liberal democratic societies tend to enjoy greater health, more trade, richer exchanges of ideas and other large blessings.

The development of diverse democratic institutions in the states of the former Soviet Empire represented here tonight is an example of the process at work.

The political development of your countries demonstrates how democracy can conduce to peace—how it can create states that become stronger, safer and more prosperous, without threatening their neighbors.

Building Democracy In Iraq Has Helped Stamp Out Terrorism

This is also what we hope to achieve in Iraq.

The adoption last fall of our timetable to turn over sovereign authority to the Iraqis on July 1, 2004 has been useful in stimulating political reconstruction in Iraq.

The coalition's strategic aim in Iraq is to put the Iraqis in a position to run their own country. The US has no desire whatever to run Iraq, let alone (as the conspiracy mongers allege) to exploit it.

Strategic success will be Iraqis creating for themselves an Iraq that gives freedom and prosperity to its own people and does not threaten its neighbors or others.

The setting of deadlines—for example, the end of February [2004] deadline for the adoption of the so-called Iraqi interim constitution and the end of June [2004] deadline for the handover of sovereign authority—has had the intended effect of encouraging Iraqis to become more

The Freedom Quilt in Washington DC is one of many American symbols that inspire people all around the world to support democracy.

active in running their own ministries and in getting work completed in the Iraqi Governing Council.

The interim constitution, which was completed only three days after the deadline, is an admirable document, the fruit of impressive political skill and the art of compromise on the part of the Iraqi Governing Council.

Iraqis have stepped forward to manage the health ministry, the oil ministry and other key national ministries. And Iraqis are doing good work in the over 250 local governing councils also.

We Cannot Defeat Terrorism Without Democracy

As President Bush has recently reaffirmed, the United States will see our mission through in Iraq. Success in Iraq can contribute importantly to success in the war on terrorism generally. The building of democratic institutions in Iraq is crucial to fighting the battle of ideas within the war on terrorism. Iraq could become a model of moderation, freedom and prosperity. The stakes there are high.

Analyze the essay:

1. Feith has worked for more than twenty years in various positions in the American government or for high-ranking world leaders and institutions. Does knowing his background influence the weight you give his opinions and arguments? If so, in what way? If not, why not? Explain your reasoning.
2. Feith argues that democracy can help reduce terrorism; Dale Netherton, author of the following essay, argues that democracy cannot help reduce terrorism. After reading both essays, with which author do you agree? What ideas and pieces of evidence helped you come to your conclusion? Cite them in your answer.

Spreading Democracy Will Not Reduce Terrorism

Dale Netherton

In the following essay author Dale Netherton argues that democracy alone is not enough to reduce terrorism—and may even support it. He explains that democracy is merely the opportunity to vote and can backfire if a citizenry elects an evil or unjust government. He cites the democratic election of the terrorist group Hamas in 2006 as an example of how democracy does not automatically reduce terrorism. Using democratic channels, Palestinians put terrorists into power, and Netherton predicts it will happen elsewhere if the United States tries to impose democracy. Netherton explains that more important than imposing democratic institutions is to cultivate a respect for individualism. When the individual is valued, freedom and rights will follow. Netherton argues that it is a mistake to think that democracy can fix all of the world's problems, especially terrorism—in the wrong hands, he concludes, democracy can end up giving terrorists the legitimacy and support they crave.

Netherton is a participant in the Ayn Rand Institute's Atlantis Legacy program. He has written extensively for a variety of publications, including the *American Chronicle*, where this essay was originally published.

Consider the following questions:

1. According to Netherton, what do Nazis, Communists, and members of Hamas all have in common? How do they differ from Americans?
2. When, says Netherton, is voting bad?
3. When and only when is democracy a good fit for a society, according to Netherton?

The recent Hamas[1] victory at the polls shows us why spreading Democracy is not the answer to getting a more peaceful world.

Democratically Electing Terrorists

Just because people vote doesn't mean that what they will vote for will necessarily be positive. Voting is merely choosing an alternative and if the alternatives are false or evil then the sanction of the vote is merely more encouragement for the leader chanting aggression and war. This should be so obvious without the example of the Hamas victory as those who voted for Sadam, Stalin, etc. told the story over the centuries to those who studied and understood.

Democracy Does Not Work in Societies That Don't Value Individualism

But like the politician that spouts off about the need for price controls ignoring the forty centuries of failure of this ignorance of market manipulation, the pro-democracy fanatic thinks voting by itself will produce good people with good intentions and peaceful ways. This naive notion comes from a position that says people want a free nation with the rights of the individual protected. But people who are taught and believe that they are a part of a tribe or a group or a nation or a belief system have no idea corresponding to individualism. They are only pawns to the leaders of their group. The Nazis were a group, the Communists were a group, Hamas is a group, but Americans are individuals first and foremost and our government has been created to recognize and protect that idea.

In the Wrong Hands Democracy Will Support Terrorism

Unless the spread of democracy is rejected as insufficient to achieve a rational foreign policy we will end up creat-

1. In 2006 Palestinians held free elections and elected members of Hamas, a terrorist group.

ing more and more Hamas victories. The Fatahs [another Palestinian group with ties to terrorism] of the world will seek to create a facade that they are not terrorists and will take our money as we delude ourselves to their true nature. The riots by the Fatah after the Hamas victory shows clearly their dedication to the tenets of democracy. Democracy to them is only good as long as they win elections, stay in power and can delude the United States into sending them money and hamstringing Israel. Even the Democrats realize, so far, that even though they lose elections they cannot get their way by violence. How long that will continue is anybodies guess. But you will notice the hostility and hatred is building.

U.S. protesters advocate for peace and democracy in Lebanon and Palestine. However, democracy may not be compatible with certain societies.

Democracy Alone Cannot Create Change

Voting is good if you can have a rational choice. Voting is bad if the only alternatives are simply steps in the direction of dictatorship, loss of individual liberty and destruction of civilized behavior. But to have rational alternatives you must have rational objectives. If the objective is to fulfill an ancient

Many believe that the United States should not take on the responsibility of trying to impose democracy in other countries.

prophecy or rule the world by force or to create a society where no one can earn without having their earnings confiscated, there can be no rational alternatives except reversal of the irrational objectives. This requires creating a set of rational objectives which is more than just rejection of the irrational ones. You can't fill a void with something you disapprove of. To be for individual rights is a rational objective because it impacts everyone and serves their self interest. To be for the "rights" of the fanatics is to subjugate the rights of the individual to the power of the fanatics. This is in no one's interest. . . .

We Must Spread Rationality and Individualism

The cry of democracy is what comes from making a package deal out of a way of life that includes democracy but has more fundamental ingredients that make rational objectives and therefore rational alternatives possible. We do not need to spread democracy. We need to spread rational objectives. We need to identify and reject irrational objectives and contrast them with the rational alternatives that proceed from rational objectives. For instance, a person must be shown that if their rights of life, liberty and the pursuit of happiness with the protection of property rights gives them a chance to prosper and earn a living they can support those who advocate protecting their rights and reject those who support redistribution schemes, theocratic dynasties and welfare states. We in the United States have few rational alternatives any more because of the erosion of this

> ## Free Elections in the Middle East Will Produce Unfriendly Governments
>
> If democracy were achieved in the Middle East, what kind of governments would it produce? Would they cooperate with the United States on important policy objectives [such as] curbing terrorism, . . . advancing the Arab-Israeli peace process, maintaining security in the Persian Gulf, and ensuring steady supplies of oil? No one can predict the course a new democracy will take, but based on public opinion surveys and recent elections in the Arab world, the advent of democracy there seems likely to produce new Islamist governments that would be much less willing to cooperate with the United States than are the current authoritarian rulers.
>
> F. Gregory Gause, "Can Democracy Stop Terrorism?" *Foreign Affairs*, Sept–Oct 2005. http://www.foreign affairs.org/20050901faessay84506/f-gregory-gause-iii/can-democracy-stop-terrorism.html.

understanding. We too have bought into the notion of democracy leading us into the right direction simply by going to the polls. . . .

Democracy can only be a good fit if the rights of the individual are clearly delineated and protected. These rights cannot be protected by a dictator or a ruling committee. The governing must be freely chosen by the governed and the governing must realize theirs is a limited function that must not infringe on the rights of the governed. The rational objective must lead to rational alternatives at the ballot box. If this is not the approach democracy will be the pawn of the demagogue and the vote will be a futile gesture. An irrational vote will not elect a champion of liberty and a system that is only counting irrational votes has nothing to offer the individual, a nation or the future.

Analyze the essay:

1. Netherton argues that spreading individualism is more important than spreading democracy. Explain what he means by this. What is the difference between individualism and democracy? What happens when you have one without the other?

2. In the essay you just read, Netherton uses history, facts, and examples to make his argument that democracy will not reduce terrorism (and may even support it). He does not, however, use any quotations to support his point. If you were to rewrite this article and insert quotations, what sources might you quote from? What voices would you include? Where would you place these quotations to bolster the points Netherton makes?

Section Two:
Model Essays
and Writing
Exercises

The Five-Paragraph Essay

A n *essay* is a short piece of writing that discusses or analyzes one topic. The five-paragraph essay is a form commonly used in school assignments and tests. Every five-paragraph essay begins with an *introduction*, ends with a *conclusion*, and features three *supporting paragraphs* in the middle.

The Thesis Statement. The introduction includes the essay's thesis statement. The thesis statement presents the argument or point the author is trying to make about the topic. The essays in this book all have different thesis statements because they are making different arguments about democracy.

The thesis statement should clearly tell the reader what the essay will be about. A focused thesis statement helps determine what will be in the essay; the subsequent paragraphs are spent developing and supporting its argument.

The Introduction. In addition to presenting the thesis statement, a well-written introductory paragraph captures the attention of the reader and explains why the topic being explored is important. It may provide the reader with background information on the subject matter or feature an anecdote that illustrates a point relevant to the topic. It could also present startling information that clarifies the point of the essay or put forth a contradictory position that the essay will refute. Further techniques for writing an introduction are found later in this section.

The Supporting Paragraphs. The introduction is then followed by three (or more) supporting paragraphs. These are the main body of the essay. Each paragraph presents and develops a subtopic that supports the essay's thesis statement. Each subtopic is then supported with its own facts, details, and examples. The writer can use various kinds of supporting material and details to back up the topic of each supporting paragraph. These may include statistics, quotations from people with special knowledge or expertise, historic facts, and anecdotes. A rule of writing is that specific and concrete examples are more convincing than vague, general, or unsupported assertions.

The Conclusion. The conclusion is the paragraph that closes the essay. Its function is to summarize or reiterate the main idea of the essay. It may recall an idea from the introduction or briefly examine the larger implications of the thesis. Because the conclusion is also the last chance a writer has to make an impression on the reader, it is important that it not simply repeat what has been presented elsewhere in the essay but close it in a clear, final, and memorable way.

Although the order of the essay's component paragraphs is important, they do not have to be written in that order. Some writers like to decide on a thesis and write the introduction paragraph first. Other writers like to focus first on the body of the essay and write the introduction and conclusion later.

Pitfalls to Avoid

When writing essays about controversial issues such as democracy, it is important to remember that disputes over the material are common precisely because there are many different perspectives. Remember to state your arguments in careful and measured terms. Evaluate your topic fairly—avoid overstating negative qualities of one perspective or understating positive qualities of another. Use examples, facts, and details to support any assertions you make.

The Descriptive Essay

The previous section of this book provided you with samples of published persuasive writing on democracy. Many of these essays used description to convey their message. In this section you will focus on developing your own descriptive writing skills.

A descriptive essay gives a reader a mental picture of the subject that the writer is exploring. Typically, descriptive writing uses the five senses—sight, sound, touch, taste, and smell—to help the reader experience what the writer has experienced. A descriptive writer carefully selects vivid examples and specific details to reveal people, places, processes, events, and ideas.

Using the Descriptive Essay

While an essay can be purely descriptive, descriptive papers written for the classroom are often persuasive or expository essays that use description to make a point. Writers may also rely on description as they explain a memory or discuss an experience. For example, in Viewpoint Six, Dale Netherton describes the Nazis, the Communists, and the Palestinian terrorist group Hamas as examples of groups that cannot subscribe to democracy because of their lack of appreciation for the individual. Giving specific examples of the way in which respect for individualism goes hand in hand with democracy helps drives home the author's point.

Sometimes descriptive essays are written in the first person (from the "I" point of view). Descriptive essays are a good format for the first person because details about a particular event or experience are well delivered through a person's memories or opinions. In these cases there is usually not one sentence that can be singled out as the thesis statement. Instead the essay has an *implied* thesis—a point of view made evident through the writer's careful use of details and examples. An example of first person writing is found in Viewpoint Five by Douglas J. Feith. Feith recounts the time he served in the Reagan administration in the first person.

Descriptive Writing Techniques

An important element of descriptive writing is the use of images and specific and concrete details. Specific and concrete is the opposite of general and abstract. Descriptive writers should give their readers a fuller understanding of the topic by focusing on tangible details and by appealing to the five senses. See the accompanying box for examples of general nouns and their more specific variations.

General and Specific Descriptions

General	More Specific	Most Specific
food	pasta	linguine
fish	salmon	sockeye
errand	in the mall	specific store
feeling	happiness	elation
sound	crash	broken glass

The use of *metaphors* and *similes* can also enliven descriptive writing. A *metaphor* is a word or phrase that compares two objects. A *simile* is a metaphor that includes the prepositions *like* or *as*. In Model Essay Two, "The Patriot Act Does Not Threaten Democracy," the author uses a simile in Paragraph 4 to drive home the point that the Patriot Act did not become a law too hastily.

Some descriptive essays make use of *scene* and *exposition*. The *scene* is an element commonly found in fiction and in creative writing. With scene a writer describes an event with moment-by-moment detail, often including dialogue if people are involved. With *exposition* a writer explains, summarizes, or concisely recounts events that occur between scenes. Scene is comparable to showing, while exposition is similar to telling.

Tips to Remember

A descriptive essay should give the reader a clear impression of its subject. So a writer must select the most relevant details. A few well-chosen details are more effective than dozens of random ones. You want the reader to visualize what you are describing but not feel overloaded with information. The room you are sitting in now, for example, is likely full of many concrete and specific items. To describe the room in writing, however, you would want to choose just a few of the most vivid details that would help convey your impression of and attitude about it.

A writer should also be aware of the kinds of words he or she uses in descriptive passages. Modifying words like adjectives and adverbs can enhance descriptive writing, but they should be used sparingly. Generally, verbs and nouns are more powerful than adjectives and adverbs. The overuse of modifying words makes the writing seem wordy and unnatural. Compare the phrases in the accompanying box to see the difference between wordy and concise language.

Wordy vs. Concise Language

Wordy	Concise
furry animal with four legs and a tail	furry dog
rolling around rapidly in brilliant untamed magnificence	dancing in wild splendor
she laughed extremely loudly and with feeling	she laughed
the best most amazingly wonderful experience	a fantastic time

In the following section you will read model descriptive essays about democracy and work on exercises that will help you write your own.

The True Price of Freedom: How a Lack of Democracy Causes Terrorism

Editor's Notes The first model essay argues that a lack of democracy is a key contributor to terrorism. The author explains why she believes there is a link between lack of democracy and terrorism and describes how nations that are not free are uniquely vulnerable to terrorism. The essay is structured as a five-paragraph descriptive essay in which each paragraph contributes a supporting piece of evidence to develop the argument. The author uses descriptive techniques to make her ideas specific and vivid; she also uses persuasive techniques to convince you of her argument.

The notes in the margin point out key features of the essay and will help you understand how the essay is organized. Also note that all sources are cited using Modern Language Association (MLA) style.* For more information on how to cite your sources, see Appendix C. In addition, consider the following questions:

1. How does the introduction engage the reader's attention?
2. What descriptive techniques are used in the essay?
3. What purpose do the essay's quotes serve?
4. Does the essay convince you of its point?

> Refers to thesis and topic sentences

> Refers to supporting details

Paragraph 1

It is often said that poverty causes terrorism. On the surface, it seems logical to think that those who are poor would violently lash out against richer people. After all, consider for a moment what it is like to live in one of the poorest countries in the world: You don't have access to

---

* In applying MLA style, the following simplifications have been made: Parenthetical text citations are confined to direct quotations only; electronic source documentation in the Works Cited lists omits dates of access, page ranges, and some detailed facts of publication.

These specific, descriptive details help you picture what it is like to live in a poor country. Always use specific rather than vague details when writing.

clean water, electricity, or fresh foods. You may live three or four to a bedroom, and live in a house with dirt walls and flooring. You may have to walk for miles to the nearest village, store, or water well. Watching richer nations grow richer every day could inspire you to commit terrorism against their citizens and resources. This very scenario has been described by many high-profile politicians and academics to explain what motivates terrorists to commit their deadly acts. But on closer inspection, it appears that terrorism is not a reaction to poverty, but a reaction to how free a people are and whether their nation practices democracy.

This is the essay's thesis statement. It tells what main point the essay will argue.

Paragraph 2

Data of those who lash out most violently—suicide bombers—show they are not overwhelmingly poor. A 2003 Princeton University study by Claude Berrebi, for example, found that only 13 percent of Palestinian suicide bombers come from impoverished families. Berrebi also found that 57 percent of Palestinian suicide bombers have beyond a high school education (much higher than other Palestinians; just 15 percent of non-suicide-bomber Palestinians in the same age group have beyond a high school education). This means that those Palestinians who choose to become suicide bombers are among the better educated and least poor Palestinians. Says Egyptian professor Aleya El Bindari-Hammad, "Many suicide bombers come from relatively educated, middle-class backgrounds and are not direct victims of material desperation" (24).

This is the topic sentence of paragraph 2. It is a subset of the essay's thesis. It tells what specific point this paragraph will be about.

Note how this quote supports the ideas discussed in the paragraph. It also comes from a reputable source.

Paragraph 3

Still other terrorists have been some of the richest people in the whole world. Indeed, other evidence that indicates poverty does not breed terrorism comes from the most famous terrorist attack of all time—the September 11 attacks on the United States. Indeed, fifteen of the nineteen hijackers came from Saudi Arabia, one of the wealthiest countries in the world. These men grew up in middle-

This is the topic sentence of paragraph 3. Note that all of the paragraph's details fit with it—or *support* it.

class, and even rich, households. Their lives were marked not by corrugated rooftops, tattered clothes, and utility outages. Instead, they had access to the best schools, the fanciest silk shirts, and the most delicious and freshest of foods. Furthermore, Osama bin Laden, al Qaeda leader and mastermind of many of the most deadly and shocking terrorist attacks of all time, is a billionaire (and from Saudi Arabia). Clearly these terrorists were not motivated by poverty, as conventional wisdom would think. As economics professor Alan B. Krueger has observed of terrorists in the Middle East, Latin America, and elsewhere, "Terrorists are drawn from society's elites, not the dispossessed" (C2).

> The author uses descriptive techniques to paint a picture of the 9/11 hijackers.

> Why has the author included Alan B. Krueger's job title?

Paragraph 4

Furthermore, if poverty were a key cause of terrorism, all the world's poor nations would demonstrate some connection to terrorism. But there are many poor countries that have no connection to terrorism. Honduras, Madagascar, and Ghana—three of the poorest countries in the world—have no problem with terrorists, for example. On the other hand, Saudi Arabia and Bahrain, among the world's richest countries, have spawned many terrorists and also been the site of multiple terrorist attacks. These facts have caused writers such as Salil Tripathi to reject the notion that poverty causes terrorism. "Think of the millions of poor people who live in abject conditions in Africa and Asia. Many of these countries have experienced strife and violence. But the poor there do not routinely blow up buses or turn their bodies into bombs" (Tripathi).

> How is the topic of paragraph 4 different, but related, to the other topics discussed thus far?

> "On the other hand" is a transitional phrase. It keeps the sentences linked together and keeps ideas moving.

Paragraph 5

Indeed, the factor that influences terrorism more than poverty is democracy, or how free a nation is. Research by Professor Krueger, who has surveyed international terrorist attacks through the years, shows that a country's level of civil liberties, freedom, and democracy directly correlates to its involvement in terrorism. The extent to

> This is the topic sentence of paragraph 5 and the essay's conclusion.

What details are included to support this paragraph's topic? Are they convincing to you?

which a nation's citizens are free to develop opinions, create political institutions, and cultivate personal autonomy without interference from the government have the most bearing on whether they will become involved with, or support, terrorism. Studies by the Freedom House—an organization that measures freedom and democracy around the world—similarly show that income and living conditions bear no relation to involvement in terrorism. Instead, Freedom House ranks wealthy, terrorist-sponsoring nations such as Saudi Arabia as "not free" based on its repression of political rights, speech, civil liberties, electoral process, rule of law, and other categories. Clearly, then, "the freedom to assemble and protest peacefully without interference from the government goes a long way to providing an alternative to terrorism" (Krueger C2). To this end, the United States should focus on fostering democracy in places where citizens are suppressed if it wants to eradicate a root cause of terrorism.

The author includes a "call to action" in her conclusion. A call to action is when, based on the information presented, the author advises a course of action.

Works Cited

El Bindari-Hammad, Aleya. "Defusing the Humiliation Bomb." *For a Change* Oct.–Nov. 2005: 24.

Krueger, Alan B. "Cash Rewards and Poverty Alone Do Not Explain Terrorism." *New York Times* 29 May 2003: C2.

Tripathi, Salil. "Debunking the Poverty-Terrorism Myth." *Asian Wall Street Journal* 23 Feb. 2005.

Exercise 1A: Create an Outline from an Existing Essay

It often helps to create an outline of the five-paragraph essay before you write it. The outline can help you organize the information, arguments, and evidence you have gathered during your research.

For this exercise, create an outline that could have been used to write "The True Price of Freedom: How a Lack of Democracy Causes Terrorism." This "reverse engineering" exercise is meant to help familiarize you with how outlines can help classify and arrange information.

To do this you will need to

1. articulate the essay's thesis
2. pinpoint important pieces of evidence
3. flag quotes that supported the essay's ideas, and
4. identify key points that supported the argument.

Part of the outline has already been started to give you an idea of the assignment.

Outline

I. **Paragraph 1:**
   A. Write the essay's thesis: Rather than being a reaction to poverty, terrorism is a reaction to how free a people are and whether their nation practices democracy.

II. **Paragraph 2:**
   A. Topic:

      i. Princeton University study that found that only 13 percent of Palestinian suicide bombers come from impoverished families, and in general have a high level of education compared to others their age.
      ii. Quote by Egyptian professor Aleya El Bindari-Hammad that confirms that suicide bombers tend to be well educated and not poor.

III. Paragraph 3:
   A. Topic: Terrorists have been some of the richest people in the world.

   i.

   ii.

IV. Paragraph 4:
   A. Topic:

   i. Honduras, Madagascar, and Ghana–three of the poorest countries in the world–have no problem with terrorists.
   ii. Salil Tripathi quote that argues against the notion that poverty causes terrorism.

V. Paragraph 5:
   A. Write the essay's conclusion:

Exercise 1B: Create an Outline for Your Own Essay

The first model essay expresses a particular point of view about democracy. For this exercise, your assignment is to find supporting ideas, choose specific and concrete details, create an outline, and ultimately write a five-paragraph essay making a different, or even opposing, point about democracy. Your goal is to use descriptive techniques to convince your reader.

Part I: Write a thesis statement.

The following thesis statement would be appropriate for an essay on why democracies are uniquely vulnerable to terrorism:

Democracies are uniquely vulnerable to terrorism because they are open and free—the nature of such a society makes it infinitely easier for terrorists to move freely, plot in secrecy, and attack the open, unguarded systems that are available to the public.

Or, see the sample paper topics suggested in Appendix D for more ideas.

Part II: Brainstorm pieces of supporting evidence.

Using information found in this book and from your own research, write down three arguments or pieces of evidence that support the thesis statement you selected. Then, for each of these three arguments, write down facts, examples, and details that support it. These could be:

- statistical information
- personal memories and anecdotes
- quotes from experts, peers, or family members
- observations of people's actions and behaviors
- specific and concrete details

Supporting pieces of evidence for the above sample thesis statement include:

- The fact that people who live in democracies travel freely on trains, buses, subways, and airplanes; enjoy a high level of privacy; and are granted personal liberties such as free speech and the right to a fair trial—each of these makes it easier for terrorists to hatch plots in secrecy.
- Terrorism expert Robert A. Pape has documented democratic nations' vulnerability to terrorism. He writes, "The United States, France, India, Israel, Russia, Sri Lanka, and Turkey have been the targets of almost every suicide attack of the past two decades, and each country has been a democracy at the time of the incidents." Read more on Pape's views about democracy and terrorism in his book, *Dying to Win* (Robert A. Pape, *Dying to Win: The Strategic Logic of Suicide Terrorism.* New York: Random House, 2005).

Part III: Place the information from Part I in outline form.

Part IV: Write the arguments or supporting statements in paragraph form.

By now you have three arguments that support the essay's thesis statement, as well as supporting material. Use the outline to write out your three supporting arguments in paragraph form. Make sure each paragraph has a topic sentence that states the paragraph's thesis clearly and broadly. Then, add supporting sentences that express the facts, quotes, details, and examples that support the paragraph's argument. The paragraph may also have a concluding or summary sentence.

The Patriot Act Does Not Threaten Democracy

Editor's Notes The second model essay argues that the Patriot Act does not threaten democracy. Like the first model essay, it is both a descriptive essay and a persuasive essay: The author uses *descriptive* techniques to *persuade* her readers to agree with her point of view. The essay is structured as a five-paragraph essay in which each paragraph contributes a supporting piece of evidence to develop the argument.

Like you did for the first model essay, take note of the essay's components and how they are organized (the sidebars in the margins will help you identify the essay's pieces and their purpose).

■ Refers to thesis and topic sentences

■ Refers to supporting details

Paragraph 1

Secret, warrantless searches. Innocent men and women carted away in the middle of the night by nameless authorities. Taped conversations. Cameras watching your every move. These are but a few of the images that come to mind when critics of the Patriot Act talk of America's most important antiterrorism law. Indeed, opponents of the Patriot Act have made it out to be a draconian piece of legislation that threatens to turn America into a fascist state. But the hysteria over the Patriot Act is unwarranted and inaccurate; in no way do the provisions of the act undermine America's democracy or threaten its commitment to preserving civil liberties.

The essay begins with specific, descriptive details meant to grab your attention.

This is the essay's thesis statement. All of the material in the essay is related to proving this point.

Paragraph 2

One Patriot Act provision that generates needless controversy is Section 215. This section allows federal terrorism investigators access to records that help them conduct a criminal investigation. Through Section 215 they can access a suspect's driver's license records, for example, or view school enrollments or purchases made as

What is the topic sentence of paragraph 2?

71

they relate to the criminal investigation. Section 215 does not give authorities carte blanche to go through any and all of a person's records. In fact, it merely expands on the already existing—and legal—right of courts to demand that businesses hand over records relevant to criminal investigations. Fears that authorities will use Section 215 to get access to unrelated private records, or to spy on what they purchase, are completely unwarranted. Viet D. Dinh, who, as former assistant attorney general for the Office of Legal Policy oversaw the drafting and implementation of the first version of the Patriot Act, assures Americans that Section 215 could never be used for such a gross violation of privacy. "The records of average Americans, and even not-so average criminals, are simply beyond the reach of Section 215" (Dinh 4).

Note Dinh's qualifications. What made the author choose to quote him?

Paragraph 3

Critics are equally hysterical about Section 213 of the Patriot Act, which grants authorities the ability to conduct searches in a way that will not alert parties under suspicion to the fact that they are under surveillance. Section 213 allows law enforcement to postpone delivering a search warrant to a suspect until after a search has been conducted. They are granted authority to do this if there is a threat to life or physical safety (i.e., if a terrorist attack is imminent); if a suspect is a flight risk; or if it seems likely that a suspect will tamper with evidence if notified beforehand of a search. Section 213 makes good sense in the context of the war on terrorism. Authorities cannot tell a suspected terrorist that they will be coming to inspect their apartment for weapons of mass destruction on Tuesday at 10:00 A.M. To catch terrorists, authorities must have the advantage of the element of surprise. Furthermore, it is hard to see how Section 213 could constitute an upset to liberty and democracy, especially compared with other laws. "On the scale of threats to liberty, Section 213 ranks far, far below such widely ignored laws as, for example, the five-year mandatory minimum prison sentence for possessing five grams of crack cocaine" (Taylor).

What is the topic sentence of paragraph 3? How does it relate to the essay's thesis statement?

What pieces of this essay are opinions? What parts are facts? Make a list of opinions and facts and see which the author relies on more.

What point in paragraph 3 does this quote support?

Paragraph 4

A final way in which the Patriot Act does not undermine democracy is evidenced by the very process through which it was developed. The laws of the Patriot Act were not dreamed up behind closed doors or imposed overnight by a secret police. The Patriot Act's provisions were written, debated, and voted on by America's elected leaders. Debates took place out in the open, with a written trail of statements and testimonies. The way critics talk, one would think the Patriot Act descended on Americans like a flash flood or deadly midnight hurricane. But "contrary to popular myth, the Patriot Act was not rushed onto the statute books. During the six weeks of deliberations that led to the passage of the Act, the drafters heard from, and heeded the advice of, a coalition of concerned voices urging caution and care in crafting the blueprint for America's security" (Dinh 3). Furthermore, senators and congresspeople debated for months before deciding to renew the Act in 2006. Indeed, the heated, public, and multifaceted debate that has accompanied the Patriot Act's passing and renewal only proves the health and strength of America's democratic values.

This is the topic sentence of paragraph 4. It explores a different facet of the essay's thesis than the other paragraphs.

The author uses a simile to argue that the Patriot Act did not become a law too hastily. For more on similes and other descriptive techniques see Preface B.

This sentence reiterates the topic of paragraph 4, bringing the point home in a strong and memorable way.

Paragraph 5

Instead of a draconian set of laws that undermine America's democracy, the Patriot Act helps protect the country from terrorist attack while respecting the democratic values that make America worth defending. Most Americans realize that in the war on terror, they must strike the right balance between liberty and security. No one wants an America in which secret searches and midnight detainments are commonplace, or one in which mechanical eyes and ears watch our every move. The Patriot Act provides us with commonsense security laws that protect our democracy by making such extreme measures unnecessary. Critics of the Patriot Act would do well to reserve their hysteria for real threats to democracy.

Note how the author returns to ideas introduced in paragraph 1. See Exercise A for more on introductions and conclusions.

Works Cited

Dinh, Viet D. "How the USA Patriot Act Defends Democracy." Foundation for the Defense of Democracies 1 Jun. 2004. < www.defenddemocracy.org/usr_doc/USA_Patriot_Act_2.pdf > .

Taylor, Jr., Stuart. "Patriot Act Hysteria Meets Reality." *Atlantic* 19 Apr. 2005.

Exercise 2A: Examining Introductions and Conclusions

Every essay features introductory and concluding paragraphs that are used to frame the main ideas being presented. Along with presenting the essay's thesis statement, well-written introductions should grab the attention of the reader and make clear why the topic being explored is important. The conclusion reiterates the essay's thesis and is also the last chance for the writer to make an impression on the reader. Strong introductions and conclusions can greatly enhance an essay's effect on an audience.

The Introduction

There are several techniques that can be used to craft an introductory paragraph. An essay can start with:

- an anecdote: a brief story that illustrates a point relevant to the topic;
- startling information: facts or statistics that elucidate the point of the essay;
- setting up and knocking down a position: a position or claim believed by proponents of one side of a controversy, followed by statements that challenge that claim;
- historical perspective: an example of the way things used to be that leads into a discussion of how or why things work differently now;
- summary information: general introductory information about the topic that feeds into the essay's thesis statement.

Problem One

Reread the introductory paragraphs of the model essays and of the viewpoints in Section One. Identify which of the techniques described above are used in the example essays. How do they grab the attention of the reader? Are their thesis statements clearly presented?

Problem Two

Write an introduction for the essay you have outlined and partially written in Exercise 1B using one of the techniques described above.

The Conclusion

The conclusion brings the essay to a close by summarizing or returning to its main ideas. Good conclusions, however, go beyond simply repeating these ideas. Strong conclusions explore a topic's broader implications and reiterate why it is important to consider. They may frame the essay by returning to an anecdote featured in the opening paragraph. Or, they may close with a quotation or refer to an event in the essay. In opinionated essays, the conclusion can reiterate which side the essay is taking or ask the reader to reconsider a previously held position on the subject.

Problem Three

Reread the concluding paragraphs of the model essays and of the viewpoints in Section One. Which were most effective in driving their arguments home to the reader? What sorts of techniques did they use to do this? Did they appeal emotionally to the reader, or bookend an idea or event referenced elsewhere in the essay?

Problem Four

Write a conclusion for the essay you have outlined and partially written in Exercise 1B using one of the techniques described above.

Exercise 2B: Using Quotations to Enliven Your Essay

No essay is complete without quotations. Get in the habit of using quotes to support at least some of the ideas in your essays. Quotes do not need to appear in every paragraph, but often enough so that the essay contains voices aside from your own. When you write, use quotations to accomplish the following:

- Provide expert advice that you are not necessarily in the position to know about
- Cite lively or passionate passages
- Include a particularly well-written point that gets to the heart of the matter

- Supply statistics or facts that have been derived from someone's research
- Deliver anecdotes that illustrate the point you are trying to make
- Express first-person testimony

There are a couple of important things to remember when using quotations:

- Note your sources' qualifications and biases. This way your reader can identify the person you have quoted and can put their words in a context.
- Put any quoted material within proper quotation marks. Failing to attribute quotes to their authors constitutes plagiarism, which is when an author takes someone else's words or ideas and presents them as his or her own. Plagiarism is a very serious infraction and must be avoided at all costs.

Problem One
Reread the essays presented in all sections of this book and find at least one example of each of the above quotation types.

Democracy Denied? An Investigation of the 2004 Elections

The last model essay explores the presidential election of 2004. It argues that some American voters were disenfranchised, or denied their legal right to vote. Unlike the previous model essays, the following essay is more than five paragraphs. Sometimes five paragraphs are simply not enough to develop an idea adequately. Extending the length of an essay can allow the reader to explore a topic in more depth or present multiple pieces of evidence that together provide a complete picture of a topic. Longer essays can also help readers discover the complexity of a subject by examining a topic beyond its superficial exterior. Moreover, the ability to write a sustained research or position paper is a valuable skill you will need as you advance academically.

The following essay also differs from the first two model essays in that it required the author to conduct personal interviews in order to report on an event. See Exercises 3A and 3B for more information on conducting interviews and reporting on events.

As you read the following essay, take note of the sidebars in the margin. Pay attention to how it is organized and presented.

Refers to thesis and topic sentences

Refers to supporting details

Paragraph 1

A fundamental pillar of the American democracy is our electoral system. Elections in the United States are supposed to be free, private, and fair, and all those who are eligible to vote are supposed to have the right to do so. But the 2004 presidential elections were plagued with problems that caused America's commitment to democracy to come under question. Troubles with ballots, voting machines, and registered voter lists may have robbed some Americans of their right to vote. An investigation of

What is the essay's thesis statement?

78

these issues allows us to assess the health of democracy in America and reminds us of just how important free and fair elections are to our society.

Paragraph 2

One of the ways in which the 2004 elections robbed some Americans of their right to vote was in the absentee ballot process. Absentee ballots are supposed to allow those Americans living outside the country the chance to have their vote counted in absentia. Instead of showing up at the polls on election day, those living abroad fill out absentee ballots and send them by mail by a certain date to be counted in the general election. But in the 2004 elections, half of the 6 million American voters living abroad either never received their ballots or received them too late to vote. The result was that Americans who found themselves living abroad were denied their right to participate in their country's election.

> What is the topic sentence of paragraph 2? How do you recognize it?

Paragraph 3

Kelly Ryan, a California resident who was living abroad in Germany in 2004, is just one of hundreds of thousands of Americans living abroad who were denied their right to participate in their country's political process. Ryan remembers the frustrating process of trying to vote from far away. "Absentee voting is always a little difficult. You must plan well in advance to make sure your ballot shows up in time, and it helps to have access to a P.O. box, which I did. But I had to put in three different requests for my absentee ballot to show up," she said. "When it finally did, it was so close to the deadline that I doubted whether it would get home in time to be counted" (qtd. in Friedman). Ryan was disheartened by the idea of her vote arriving home too late to be factored into the tallying process. "It was, more than ever, important to me that my vote be counted," said Ryan. "Living abroad made me realize how special the American system of democracy is. So it was endlessly disappointing to feel the process working against me and my rights" (qtd. in Friedman).

> What do Ryan's quotes lend the essay? In what way do they support the main argument?

What is the topic sentence of paragraph 4?

Machine malfunctions accounted for another facet of denied democracy in the 2004 elections. According to a 2005 report undertaken by the United States Election Assistance Commission, as many as 1 million ballots across the United States were rendered void by faulty voting equipment. In some places the malfunctions occurred in such tight races that they could have made the difference between who won and lost the election. In New Mexico, for example, malfunctioning machines accidentally deleted votes for the presidential candidate on 18,997 ballots. In that state, where the presidential election was decided by just 5,988 votes, the missing votes could have altered the outcome of the election there.

What supporting details appear in paragraph 4? How do they relate to the topic sentence?

What transitional words and phrases appear in the essay? Make a list.

But no state was more important to the 2004 election than Ohio, and perhaps no American citizens were more disenfranchised than voters there. Many legal voters in Ohio were prevented from casting their votes because their names had been deleted from registered voter lists. In fact, according to an investigative report by Robert F. Kennedy Jr., "in Cleveland Ohio, nearly one in four voter names were wiped from the voting registers between 2000 and 2004. . . . In Cleveland's precinct 6C, more than half the voters on the rolls were deleted" (47). In some cases the deletions were legitimate—names were deleted if they belonged to people who had moved or died since the 2000 election and thus no longer had a right to vote in Ohio.

What makes Robert F. Kennedy Jr. qualified to speak on this topic?

What is the topic sentence of paragraph 6? How does it relate to the essay's thesis?

But many people who were legally registered to vote also had their names deleted, a violation of their rights. Officials mistook people who had not voted in the 2000 election for being ineligible to vote in the 2004 election and wiped their names from registered voter lists. According to a House of Representatives report that investigated the election proceedings in Ohio, illegal deletions on voter registration lists "likely disenfranchised tens of thousands of voters statewide" (Conyers 6). Kennedy estimates that

What details support the main idea of paragraph 6?

about thirty thousand Ohio citizens were unfairly denied their opportunity to vote due to this glitch.

Paragraph 7

One such person denied her right to vote in this way was Ohio resident Jordan Cowan. Cowan had been registered to vote in Ohio in 2000, but had refrained from casting a ballot due to a lack of interest in the political process. Come 2004, however, she realized that the right to vote is something she did not want to take for granted. Said Cowan, "Seeing what the people in Iraq have gone through to get the chance to vote in free elections made me realize I shouldn't take my right to vote for granted. I need to exercise it whenever I get the chance" (qtd. in Friedman). But when Cowan arrived at her polling station to cast her vote in the 2004 election, she found that her name had been deleted from the list. Said Cowan, "I was crushed. I took democracy for granted, and I guess the lesson is that even in America, democracy is something you have to fight for and protect—it's not just going to happen on its own" (qtd. in Friedman).

> Note how the author uses Cowan's account of her voting experience to support the essay's thesis and to personalize the problem of voter disenfranchisement.

Paragraph 8

It continues to be debated to what extent these problems affected the 2004 presidential race. Some, such as reporter Ted Diadiun, acknowledge that there were problems with the election but argue none were so severe as to affect the outcome of the election. "There was no shortage of mistakes made in vote counting. . . . All these mistakes and misjudgments took votes from both candidates, but . . . they didn't add up to nearly enough votes to swing Ohio from [President George W.] Bush to [Democratic candidate John] Kerry" (A2). Indeed, it is quite possible that John Kerry would never have been elected as America's forty-third president even if the election had gone smoothly.

> What is the main idea of paragraph 8?

Paragraph 9

But in a way, it shouldn't matter. Even if mistakes in the election process have no bearing on who is ultimately

What opinion is presented in paragraph 9?

elected, they should be viewed as unacceptable, and even dangerous to the American way. As Robert F. Kennedy Jr. has written, "The single greatest threat to our democracy is the insecurity of our voting system. If people lose faith that their votes are accurately and faithfully recorded, they will abandon the ballot box. Nothing less is at stake here than the entire idea of a government by the people" (56). Indeed, even if just one American was robbed of his or her right to vote, that is too many, and America must strive for better.

Paragraph 10

Troubles with ballots, voting machines, and registered voter lists were just a few of the problems in the 2004 presidential elections that caused America's commitment to democracy to come under question. Future elections must run smoother in order to maintain the public's faith in the democratic system. All Americans must be committed to protecting free, fair elections so the United States can continue to be regarded as the greatest democracy on earth.

Note how the essay's conclusion wraps up the topic in a final, memorable way—without repeating the points made in the essay.

Works Cited

Conyers, John Jr. "Preserving Democracy: What Went Wrong in Ohio: Status Report of the House Judiciary Committee Democratic Staff." 5 Jan 2005. < www.house.gov/judiciary_democrats/ohiostatusrept1505.pdf > .

Cowan, Jordan, interviewed by Lauri S. Friedman, 10 Sept. 2007.

Diadiun, Ted. "Rest Assured, We Checked Out Election 2004 Thoroughly." *Plain Dealer* (Cleveland, OH) 18 Jun. 2006: A2.

Kennedy, Robert F. Jr. "Was the 2004 Election Stolen?" Rolling Stone 15 Jun 2006. < www.rollingstone.com/news/story/10432334/was_the_2004_election-stolen > .

Ryan, Kelly, interviewed by Lauri S. Friedman, 19 Sept. 2007.

Exercise 3A: Conducting an Interview

Model Essay Three, "Democracy Denied? An Investigation of the 2004 Elections," was written after conducting interviews with people who had experienced problems while voting in the 2004 election. When reporting on events that occur in your community, you will probably need to interview people to get critical information and opinions. Interviews allow you to get the story behind a participant's experiences, enabling you to provide a fuller picture of the event.

The key to a successful interview is asking the right questions. You want the respondent to answer in as much detail as possible so you can write an accurate, colorful, and interesting piece. Therefore, you should have a clear idea of what general pieces of information you want to find out from the respondent before you begin interviewing. The six classic journalist questions—who, what, when, where, why, and how—are an excellent place to begin. If you get answers to each of these questions, you will end up with a pretty good picture of the event that took place.

There are many ways to conduct an interview, but the following suggestions will help you get started:

Step One: Choose a setting with little distraction.

Avoid bright lights or loud noises, and make sure the person you are interviewing feels comfortable speaking to you. Professional settings such as offices, places of business, and homes are always appropriate settings for an interview. If it is a phone interview, be sure you can clearly hear what the person is saying (so do not conduct the interview on a cell phone while walking on a busy city block, for example).

Step Two: Explain who you are and what you intend to learn from the interview.

Identify yourself. For what publication are you writing? If you are writing for a school paper, identify the paper. If you are conducting research for an ongoing project, explain the project's goals and in what way you expect the interviewee can help you reach them. Indicate how long you expect the interview to take, and get all contact information up front.

Step Three: Ask specific questions, and start at the beginning.

Make sure you ask at least two questions that address each of the following ideas: who, what, where, when, why, and how. Who was involved in the event? What happened during the course of the event? Where did it take place? Specific questions will change depending on what type of event you are covering. Follow your instincts; if you don't know something or have a question, ask. The answer will likely yield good information that will enhance your report.

Step Four: Take notes.

Never rely on your memory when conducting an interview. Either type or jot down notes, or ask permission to tape or otherwise record the interview.

Step Five: Verify quotes and information.

Before you write your report, it is important to go back to your source to double-check key points of information. Also, you must run any quotes you intend to use by the source before you put them in your report. This is to make sure you heard the person accurately and are not misrepresenting their position.

Types of Questions to Ask During an Interview

Questions you will ask your interviewee tend to fall in a few basic categories.

Knowledge—what they know about the topic or event. This can include historical background, logistics, and outcomes of an event. For example, Kelly Ryan in Model Essay Three provided the interviewer with information about the process of casting absentee ballots from abroad.

Sensory—ask questions about what people have seen, touched, heard, tasted, or smelled. These details will help your readers vividly imagine the event you are reporting on.

Behavior—what motivated the person to become involved in this project or movement? What do they hope to gain by having their story publicized?

Opinions, values, and feelings—ask what the person thinks about the topic or event. These questions result in opinionated or personal statements that you, as an objective reporter, most likely will not make in your report. For example, in Model Essay Three, Jordan Cowan described being "crushed" by not being able to vote and expressed her disappointment in the electoral system in a way that would be inappropriate for an objective reporter to do.

Exercise 3B: Reporting on an Event

Reports show up in many publications—newspapers, magazines, journals, and Web logs (blogs) are just some of the places people turn to read about events and activities underway in their community. Think about the type of event you'd like to report on. It could be a trip summary; the happenings of a local or school event, such as a parade, speech, assembly, or rally; a sports game; a party; or another experience in which people are coming together to get something done. Think next about the type of publication in which your report would best appear. Trip summaries, or travelogues, make great fodder for blogs; reports on school events such as sports games or performances are best featured in the school paper.

Before you report on an event, make sure you have done thorough research. Look over all notes from your interviews. Outline a road map for your essay to follow (see exercises in this book on how to outline an essay prior to writing it). Examine where quotations, information, and other details will fit best. After you absorb and organize all the information you have collected, you are ready to write.

News reports tend to be objective, so make sure your writing style is impartial and matter-of-fact. Also, be sure to provide the reader with enough information to visualize the event, but not so much that you bombard them with unnecessary or unrelated details. Use the other writing exercises found in this book—on using quotations, writing introductions and conclusions, and gathering research—to help you write the report. Then submit it for publication!

Write Your Own Descriptive Five-Paragraph Essay

Using the information from this book, write your own five-paragraph descriptive essay that deals with a topic relating to democracy. You can use the resources in this book for information about issues relating to this topic and how to structure this type of essay.

The following steps are suggestions on how to get started.

Step One: Choose your topic.

The first step is to decide what topic to write your descriptive essay on. Is there any subject that particularly fascinates you about democracy? Is there an issue you strongly support, or feel strongly against? Is there a topic you feel personally connected to or one that you would like to learn more about? Ask yourself such questions before selecting your essay topic. Refer to Appendix D: Sample Essay Topics if you need help selecting a topic.

Step Two: Write down questions and answers about the topic.

Before you begin writing, you will need to think carefully about what ideas your essay will contain. This is a process known as *brainstorming*. Brainstorming involves asking yourself questions and coming up with ideas to discuss in your essay. Possible questions that will help you with the brainstorming process include:

- Why is this topic important?
- Why should people be interested in this topic?
- How can I make this essay interesting to the reader?
- What question am I going to address in this paragraph or essay?
- What facts, ideas, or quotes can I use to support the answer to my question?

Questions especially for descriptive essays include:

- Have I chosen a compelling story to examine?
- Have I used vivid details?
- Have I made scenes come alive for my reader?

- What qualities do my characters have? Are they interesting?
- Does my descriptive essay have a clear beginning, middle, and end?
- Does my essay evoke a particular emotion or response from the reader?

Step Three: Gather facts, ideas, and anecdotes related to your topic.

This book contains several places to find information, including the viewpoints and the appendixes. In addition, you may want to research the books, articles, and Web sites listed in Section Three or do additional research in your local library. You can also conduct interviews if you know someone who has a compelling story that would fit well in your essay.

Step Four: Develop a workable thesis statement.

Use what you have written down in steps two and three to help you articulate the main point or argument you want to make in your essay. It should be expressed in a clear sentence and make an arguable or supportable point.

Example:

Democracy is not a good fit for several of the world's cultures. This could be the thesis statement of a descriptive essay that argues that democracy is not necessarily an appropriate political system for all countries in the world, and thus the United States should not attempt to spread it. Supporting paragraphs would explore reasons why the author thinks this and include specific details of cultures that are incompatible with democracy.

Step Five: Write an outline or diagram.

1. Write the thesis statement at the top of the outline.
2. Write roman numerals I, II, and III on the left side of the page with A, B, and C under each numeral.
3. Next to each roman numeral, write down the best ideas you came up with in step three. These should

all directly relate to and support the thesis statement.

4. Next to each letter write down information that supports that particular idea.

Step Six: Write the three supporting paragraphs.

Use your outline to write the three supporting paragraphs. Write down the main idea of each paragraph in sentence form. Do the same thing for the supporting points of information. Each sentence should support the paragraph of the topic. Be sure you have relevant and interesting details, facts, and quotes. Use transitions when you move from idea to idea to keep the text fluid and smooth. Sometimes, although not always, paragraphs can include a concluding or summary sentence that restates the paragraph's argument.

Step Seven: Write the introduction and conclusion.

See Exercise 2A for information on writing introductions and conclusions.

Step Eight: Read and rewrite.

As you read, check your essay for the following:

✔ Does the essay maintain a consistent tone?

✔ Do all paragraphs reinforce your general thesis?

✔ Do all paragraphs flow from one to the other? Do you need to add transition words or phrases?

✔ Have you quoted from reliable, authoritative, and interesting sources?

✔ Is there a sense of progression throughout the essay?

✔ Does the essay get bogged down in too much detail or irrelevant material?

✔ Does your introduction grab the reader's attention?

✔ Does your conclusion reflect on any previously discussed material or give the essay a sense of closure?

✔ Are there any spelling or grammatical errors?

Section Three: Supporting Research Material

Facts About Democracy

These facts can be used in reports to reinforce or add credibility when making important points.

Democracy In the World

The Economist Intelligence Unit (EIU) measures democracy across five categories: free elections, civil liberties, functioning government, political participation, and political culture. According to the EIU:

- Sweden is the most perfectly functioning democracy in the world, ranking first across all categories.

- The United States is ranked seventeenth due to lower scores in the "functioning government" and "political participation" categories.

- Twenty-eight countries are considered "full democracies"—meaning they have high marks in free elections, civil liberties, functioning government, political participation, and political culture. They include (shared rank indicates equal marks across the scored categories):

1. Sweden	15. Malta
2. Iceland	16. Spain
3. Netherlands	17. United States
4. Norway	18. Czech Republic
5. Denmark	19. Portugal
6. Finland	20. Belgium
7. Luxembourg	20. Japan
8. Australia	22. Greece
9. Canada	23. UK
10. Switzerland	24. France
11. New Zealand	25. Mauritius
11. Ireland	25. Costa Rica
13. Germany	27. Slovenia
14. Austria	27. Uruguay

- Fifty-four countries are considered "flawed democracies"—meaning these nations have some trappings of democracy, such as elections, or the right to assembly, but these rights and institutions are flawed, limited, or otherwise incomplete.

29. South Africa
30. Chile
31. South Korea
32. Taiwan
33. Estonia
34. Italy
35. India
36. Botswana
36. Cyprus
38. Hungary
39. Cape Verde
39. Lithuania
41. Slovakia
42. Brazil
43. Latvia
44. Panama
45. Jamaica
46. Poland
47. Israel
48. Trinidad and Tobago
49. Bulgaria
50. Romania
51. Croatia
52. Ukraine
53. Mexico
54. Argentina
55. Serbia
56. Mongolia
57. Sri Lanka
58. Montenegro
59. Namibia
59. Papua New Guinea
61. Suriname
62. Moldova
63. Lesotho
63. Philippines
65. Indonesia
65. Timor Leste
67. Colombia
68. Macedonia
69. Honduras
70. El Salvador
71. Paraguay
71. Benin
73. Guyana
74. Dominican Republic
75. Bangladesh
76. Peru
77. Guatemala
78. Hong Kong
79. Palestinian Territories
80. Mali
81. Malaysia
81. Bolivia

- Thirty nations are labeled as "hybrid democracies"—meaning they do not have free elections, few civil liberties, poorly functioning government, low political participation, and a poor political culture.

83. Albania	98. Liberia
84. Singapore	99. Tanzania
85. Madagascar	100. Uganda
85. Lebanon	101. Kenya
87. Bosnia and Hercegovina	102. Russia
88. Turkey	103. Malawi
89. Nicaragua	104. Georgia
90. Thailand	105. Cambodia
91. Fiji	106. Ethiopia
92. Ecuador	107. Burundi
93. Venezuela	108. Gambia
94. Senegal	109. Haiti
95. Ghana	110. Armenia
96. Mozambique	111. Kyrgyzstan
97. Zambia	112. Iraq

- Fifty-five nations are considered to be "authoritarian," meaning they rank so low in each of the five categories they cannot be considered democratic by any measure.

113. Pakistan
113. Jordan
115. Comoros
115. Morocco
115. Egypt
118. Rwanda
119. Burkina Faso
120. Kazakhstan
121. Sierra Leone
122. Niger
123. Bahrain
124. Cuba
124. Nigeria
126. Nepal
127. Côte d'Ivoire
128. Belarus
129. Azerbaijan
130. Cameroon
131. Congo Brazzaville
132. Algeria
133. Mauritania
134. Kuwait
135. Afghanistan
135. Tunisia
137. Yemen
138. China
139. Swaziland
140. Iran

141. Sudan
142. Qatar
143. Oman
144. Democratic Republic of Congo
145. Vietnam
146. Gabon
147. Bhutan
147. Zimbabwe
149. Tajikistan
150. UAE
151. Angola
152. Djibouti
153. Syria
154. Eritrea
155. Laos
156. Equatorial Guinea
157. Guinea
158. Guinea-Bissau
159. Saudi Arabia
160. Uzbekistan
161. Libya
162. Turkmenistan
163. Myanmar
164. Togo
165. Chad
166. Central Africa
167. North Korea

According to Freedom House, an American organization that tracks global trends in political freedom in less detail than the EIU:

- At the end of 2005 there were 122 "electoral democracies" (64 percent of the world's states, compared with 40 percent in the mid-1980s).
- Eighty-nine of these were rated as "politically free"— 46 percent of all states, compared with only 25 percent in 1975.

American Opinions of Democracy

- According to a Chicago Council on Global Affairs poll, Americans do not think it is as important to bring democracy to other nations as they have in the past. The poll found the following percent of Americans believe bringing democracy to other countries is:

Year	Very Important	Somewhat Important	Not Important	Not sure/ Decline
1974	28	42	22	8
1978	26	44	21	9
1982	29	47	17	7
1986	30	48	17	5
1990	28	52	17	4
1994	25	48	22	5
1998	29	50	16	5
2000	34	49	15	2
2002	24	59	16	1
2004	14	58	27	2
2006	17	57	24	2

- A February 2005 Gallup poll found 70 percent of Americans believe that "building democracy in other nations" is an important foreign policy goal, with only 31 percent saying it is very important.

- A February 2007 Third Way survey asked Americans which of the following they thought should be the main purpose of American foreign policy, and found:
    - 66 percent said "protecting the security of the United States and our allies"
    - 21 percent said "promoting freedom and democracy"
    - 9 percent said "advancing our economic interest"
    - 4 percent said "don't know"

- Most Americans do not support using military force for promoting democracy, a September 2005 PIPA–Chicago Council poll found. When asked whether they favored or opposed using military force to overthrow a dictator:
    - 35 percent favored
    - 55 percent opposed
    - 58 percent said that "using military force to overthrow a dictator does more harm than good"
    - 27 percent said that "using military force to overthrow a dictator does more good than harm"

- A February 2007 Third Way poll found that Americans are wary of believing that American democracy is superior to other democracies or systems:
    - Just 36 percent of Americans agreed with the statement "America is an exceptional nation with superior political institutions and ideals and a unique destiny to shape the world."
    - 58 percent agreed that "It is a dangerous illusion to believe America is superior to other nations; we should not be attempting to reshape other nations in light of our values."

- A PIPA–Chicago Council September 2005 poll collected American thoughts about democracy when it asked the following questions:

Do you agree or disagree with the following statement? Democracy is the best form of government.
- Agree   78%
- Disagree   15
- Don't know   7

Which position is closest to yours?
- Democracy is the best form of government for all countries   50%
- For some countries democracy is not the best form of government   43
- Don't know   6

Which of the following is closer to your view?
- People in some countries want freedom and democracy more than people in other countries   55%
- People all over the world share the desire to live in freedom and to govern themselves democratically   40
- Don't know   5

Please select which position is closer to your own views:
- When there are more democracies the world is a safer place   26%
- Democracy may make life better within a country, but it does not make the world a safer place   68
- (No answer)   6

Do you think democracies are:
- Less likely to go to war with each other than are other types of governments.   46%
- Just as likely to go to war with each other as are other types of governments.   49
- (No answer)   5

Please select which position is closer to your own views.
- Because democracies are responsive to the will of the people they are more stable and less likely to have civil wars than nondemocracies.   52%
- Because it is hard to avoid conflicts between people, democracies are just as likely to be unstable and have civil wars as nondemocracies.   41
- (No answer)   7

Do you think the United States does or does not have a responsibility to help other countries rid themselves of dictators and become democracies?
- Yes, does   56%
- No, does not   38
- No opinion   6

Do you agree or disagree with the following statement: "The United States has a moral obligation to help free other peoples from tyranny and to help create new democracies, even if that means using military force."
- Agree strongly   17%
- Agree somewhat   31
- Disagree somewhat   28
- Disagree strongly   22
- Don't know   2

Finding and Using Sources of Information

No matter what type of essay you are writing, it is necessary to find information to support your point of view. You can use sources such as books, magazine articles, newspaper articles, and online articles.

Using Books and Articles

You can find books and articles in a library by using the library's computer or cataloging system. If you are not sure how to use these resources, ask a librarian to help you. You can also use a computer to find many magazine articles and other articles written specifically for the Internet.

You are likely to find a lot more information than you can possibly use in your essay, so your first task is to narrow it down to what is likely to be most usable. Look at book and article titles. Look at book chapter titles, and examine the book's index to see if it contains information on the specific topic you want to write about. (For example, if you want to write about Islam and democracy and you find a book about political ideologies, check the chapter titles and index to be sure it contains information about Islam and democracy before you bother to check out the book.)

For a five-paragraph essay, you do not need a great deal of supporting information, so quickly try to narrow down your materials to a few good books and magazine or Internet articles. You do not need dozens. You might even find that one or two good books or articles contain all the information you need.

You probably do not have time to read an entire book, so find the chapters or sections that relate to your topic, and skim these. When you find useful information, copy it onto a note card or into a notebook. You should look for supporting facts, statistics, quotations, and examples.

Using the Internet

When you select your supporting information, it is important that you evaluate its source. This is especially important with information you find on the Internet. Because nearly anyone can put information on the Internet, there is as much bad information as good information. Before using Internet information—or any information—try to determine if the source seems to be reliable. Is the author or Internet site sponsored by a legitimate organization? Is it from a government source? Does the author have any special knowledge or training related to the topic you are looking up? Does the article give any indication of where its information comes from?

Using Your Supporting Information

When you use supporting information from a book, article, interview, or other source, there are three important things to remember:

1. *Make it clear whether you are using a direct quotation or a paraphrase.* If you copy information directly from your source, you are quoting it. You must put quotation marks around the information and tell where the information comes from. If you put the information in your own words, you are paraphrasing it.

    Here is an example of a using a quotation:

    General Wesley Clark believes that promoting democracy in the Middle East is a noble goal, but one that cannot be imposed by outside forces such as the United States. "Democracy can't be imposed—it has to be homegrown," writes Clark.

    Here is an example of a brief paraphrase of the same passage:

    General Wesley Clark believes that promoting democracy in the Middle East is a noble goal, but one that cannot be imposed by outside forces such as the United States. Clark believes that in order for democracy to truly take root, it must be embraced by local people, rather than imposed from an external culture.

2. *Use the information fairly.* Be careful to use supporting information in the way the author intended it. For example, it is unfair to quote an author as saying, "The Patriot Act is a threat to democracy," when he or she intended to say, "The Patriot Act is a threat to democracy the same way in which a kitten is a threat to a mountain lion." This is called taking information out of context. This is using supporting evidence unfairly.

3. *Give credit where credit is due.* Giving credit is known as citing. You must use citations when you use someone else's information, but not every piece of supporting information needs a citation.
   - If the supporting information is general knowledge—that is, it can be found in many sources—you do not have to cite your source.
   - If you directly quote a source, you must cite it.
   - If you paraphrase information from a specific source, you must cite it.
   - If you do not use citations where you should, you are *plagiarizing*—or stealing—someone else's work.

Citing Your Sources

There are a number of ways to cite your sources. Your teacher will probably want you to do it in one of three ways:
- Informal: As in the example in number 1 above, tell where you got the information as you present it in the text of your essay.

- Informal list: At the end of your essay, place an unnumbered list of all the sources you used. This tells the reader where, in general, your information came from.
- Formal: Use numbered footnotes or endnotes. Footnotes or endnotes are generally placed at the end of an article or essay, although they may be placed elsewhere depending on your teacher's requirements.

Works Cited

Clark, Wesley. "War Didn't and Doesn't Bring Democracy." *Washington Monthly* May 2005.

Using MLA Style to Create a Works Cited List

You will probably need to create a list of works cited for your paper. These include materials that you quoted from, relied heavily on, or consulted to write your paper. There are several different ways to structure these references. The following examples are based on Modern Language Association (MLA) style, one of the major citation styles used by writers.

Book Entries

For most book entries you will need the author's name, the book's title, where it was published, what company published it, and the year it was published. This information is usually found on the inside of the book. Variations on book entries include the following:

A book by a single author:
Afrasiabi, Kaveh. *Iran's Nuclear Program: Debating Facts Versus Fiction.* Charleston, SC: BookSurge, 2006.

Two or more books by the same author:
Friedman, Thomas L. *From Beirut to Jerusalem.* New York: Doubleday, 1989.
———. *The World Is Flat: A Brief History of the Twentieth Century.* New York: Farrar, Straus and Giroux, 2005.

A book by two or more authors:
Pojman, Louis P., and Jeffrey Reiman. *The Death Penalty: For and Against.* Lanham, MD: Rowman and Littlefield, 1998.

A book with an editor:
Friedman, Lauri S., ed. *Introducing Issues with Opposing Viewpoints: Weapons of Mass Destruction.* Farmington Hills, MI: Greenhaven, 2006.

Periodical and Newspaper Entries

Entries for sources found in periodicals and newspapers are cited a bit differently from books. For one, these sources usually have a title and a publication name. They also may have specific dates and page numbers. Unlike book entries, you do not need to list where newspapers or periodicals are published or what company publishes them.

An article from a periodical:
> Zakaria, Fareed. "Let Them Eat Carrots." *Newsweek* 23 Oct. 2004: 42.

An unsigned article from a periodical:
> "Going Critical, Defying the World." *Economist* 21 Oct. 2004: 70.

An article from a newspaper:
> McCain, John. "The War You're Not Reading About." *Washington Post* 8 Apr. 2007: B07.

Internet Sources

To document a source you found online, try to provide as much information on it as possible, including the author's name, the title of the document, date of publication or of last revision, the URL, and your date of access.

A Web source:
> Shyovitz, David. "The History and Development of Yiddish." Jewish Virtual Library. 30 May 2005. < www.jewishvirtuallibrary.org/jsource/History/ yiddish.html > .

Your teacher will tell you exactly how information should be cited in your essay. Generally, the very least information needed is the original author's name and the name of the article or other publication.

Be sure you know exactly what information your teacher requires before you start looking for your supporting information so that you know what information to include with your notes.

Sample Essay Topics

Democracy Can Prevent War

Democracy Cannot Prevent War

Democracy Is Not Appropriate for All Countries

Democracy Can Be Adopted by All Nations That Want It

Democracy Is the Best Political System

Democracy Is a Flawed Political System

Democracies Are Likely to Increase World Peace

Other Political Systems Masquerade as Democracy

Democracy Can Take Root in the Middle East

Democracy Will Be Unable to Take Root in the Middle East

Islam Is Compatible with Democracy

Islam Is Not Compatible with Democracy

America Is Committed to Promoting Democracy Around the World

America Is Not Committed to Promoting Democracy Around the World

Spreading Democracy Abroad Supports America's Foreign Policy Goals

Spreading Democracy Abroad Undermines America's Foreign Policy Goals

Spreading Democracy Abroad Will Enhance U.S. Security

Spreading Democracy Abroad Cannot Enhance U.S. Security

Building Democracies Around the World Is an Ineffective Way to Fight Terrorism

Building Democracies Around the World Is the Best Way to Fight Terrorism

The United States Should Spread Democracy by Overthrowing Dictatorships

Organizations to Contact

The editors have compiled the following list of organizations concerned with the issues debated in this book. The descriptions are derived from materials provided by the organizations. All have publications or information available for interested readers. The list was compiled on the date of publication of the present volume; names, addresses, and phone numbers may change. Be aware that many organizations take several weeks or longer to respond to inquiries, so allow as much time as possible.

American Civil Liberties Union (ACLU)

125 Broad St., 18th Floor, New York, NY 10004 • (212) 549-2500 • fax: (212) 549-2646 • e-mail: aclu@aclu.org • Web site: www.aclu.org

The ACLU is a national organization that defends Americans' civil rights guaranteed in the U.S. Constitution. It adamantly champions democracy as it pertains to issues such as free speech, human rights, and civil liberties. The ACLU offers numerous reports, fact sheets, and policy statements on a wide variety of issues, including democracy.

American Enterprise Institute (AEI)

1150 Seventeenth St. NW, Washington, DC 20036 • (202) 862-5800; (202) 862-7177 • Web site: www.aei.org

The American Enterprise Institute for Public Policy Research is a scholarly research institute that is dedicated to preserving limited government, private enterprise, and a strong foreign policy and national defense. It publishes books, including *Democratic Realism: An American Foreign Policy for a Unipolar World,* and a bimonthly magazine, *American Enterprise.*

The Brookings Institution

1775 Massachusetts Ave. NW, Washington, DC 20036 (202) 797-6000 • fax: (202) 797-6004 • e-mail: brookinfo@brook.edu • Web site: www.brookings.org

The institution, founded in 1927, is a think tank that conducts research and education in foreign policy, economics, government, and the social sciences. In 2001 it began America's Response to Terrorism, a project that provides briefings and analysis to the public and that is featured on the center's Web site. Its publishes the quarterly *Brookings Review,* periodic *Policy Briefs,* and books on the Middle East, including *Iran, Islam, and Democracy.*

Canadian Association for Free Expression (CAFE)
PO Box 332 Station B, Etobicoke, Ontario M9W 5L3, Canada
(905) 897-7221 • e-mail: cafe@canadafirst.net • Web site: www.canadianfreespeech.com

CAFE, one of Canada's leading civil liberties groups, works to strengthen the freedom of speech and freedom of expression provisions in the Canadian Charter of Rights and Freedoms. It lobbies politicians and researches threats to freedom of speech. Publications include specialized reports, leaflets, and the *Free Speech Monitor,* which is published ten times per year.

Center for Democracy and Technology (CDT)
1634 I St. NW, Suite 1100, Washington, DC 20006
(202) 637-9800 • fax: (202) 637-0968 • e-mail info@cdt.org
Web site: www.cdt.org

The mission of CDT is to develop public policy solutions that advance constitutional civil liberties and democratic values in new computer and communications media. Pursuing its mission through policy research, public education, and coalition building, the center works to increase citizens' privacy and the public's control over the use of personal information held by government and other institutions. Its publications include issue briefs, policy papers, and *CDT Policy Posts,* an online, occasional publication that covers issues regarding the civil liberties of those using the information superhighway.

Center for Responsive Politics (CRP)
1101 Fourteenth St. NW, Suite 1030, Washington, DC 20005-5635 • (202) 857-0044 • fax (202) 857-7809 • e-mail: info@crp.org • Web site: www.opensecrets.org

The CRP is a nonpartisan, nonprofit research group that tracks money in politics and its effect on elections, public policy, and democracy. The center's work is aimed at creating a more educated voter, an involved citizenry, and a more responsive government. It publishes the *Capital Eye* newsletter and numerous reports.

The Century Foundation
41 E. Seventieth St., New York, NY 10021 • (212) 535-4441 fax: (212) 879-9197 • e-mail info@tcf.org • Web site: www.tcf.org

This research foundation, formerly known as the Twentieth Century Fund, sponsors analysis of economic policy, foreign affairs, and domestic political issues. It publishes numerous books, reports, and articles, many of which focus on topics related to democracy. It also hosts project sites, including LibertyUnderAttack.org and ReformElections.org.

Council on Foreign Relations
58 E. Sixty-eighth St., New York, NY 10021 • (212) 434-9400 fax: (212) 434-9800 • e-mail: communications@cfr.org Web site: www.cfr.org

The council researches the international aspects of American economic and political policies. Its journal *Foreign Affairs,* published five times a year, provides analysis on global conflicts. Publications include "Threats to Democracy: Prevention and Response," and various articles. A video recording of the proceedings of a December 2005 conference, called "Democracy in the Arab World—Why and How," can be viewed on its Web site.

Electronic Frontier Foundation (EFF)
1550 Bryant St., Suite 725, San Francisco, CA 94103-4832 (415) 436-9333 • fax: (415) 436-9993 • e-mail: ask@eff.org Web site: www.eff.org

EFF is a nonprofit, nonpartisan organization that works to protect privacy and freedom of expression in the arena of computers and the Internet. Its missions include supporting litigation that protects First Amendment rights. EFF's Web site publishes an electronic bulletin, *Effector,* and several publications that discuss democracy and the Internet.

Freedom Forum

1101 Wilson Blvd., Arlington, VA 22209 • (703) 528-0800
(703) 284-2836 • e-mail: news@freedomforum.org
Web site: www.freedomforum.org

The Freedom Forum is an international organization that works to protect freedom of the press and free speech. It monitors developments in media and First Amendment issues on its Web site, in its monthly magazine *Forum News,* and in the *Media Studies Journal,* published twice a year.

League of Women Voters

1730 M St. NW, Suite 1000, Washington, DC 20036-4508
(202) 429-1965 • fax: (202) 429-0854 • Web site: www.lwv.org

The League of Women Voters is a private, nonpartisan political organization that works to encourage an informed and active participation of citizens in government. It provides informational materials and position papers on voter participation and campaign finance on its Web site.

National Coalition Against Censorship (NCAC)

275 Seventh Ave., New York, NY 10001 • (212) 807-6222
fax: (212) 807-6245 • e-mail: ncac@ncac.org • Web site: www.ncac.org

The coalition represents more than forty national organizations that work to prevent suppression of free speech and the press. NCAC educates the public about the dangers of censorship and how to oppose it. The coalition publishes *Censorship News* five times a year, articles, various reports, and background papers.

The National Endowment for Democracy (NED)

1101 Fifteenth St. NW, Suite 700, Washington, DC 20005
(202) 293-9072 • fax: (202) 223-6042 • e-mail: info@ned.org

The NED is a private, nonprofit organization created in 1983 to strengthen democratic institutions around the world through nongovernmental efforts. It publishes the bimonthly periodical *Journal of Democracy*.

People for the American Way (PFAW)
2000 M St. NW, Suite 400, Washington, DC 20036 • (202) 467-4999 or 1-800-326-PFAW(7329) • fax: (202) 293-2672 e-mail: pfaw@pfaw.org • Web site: www.pfaw.org

PFAW works to promote citizen participation in democracy and safeguard the principles of the U.S. Constitution, including the right to free speech. It publishes a variety of fact sheets, articles, and position statements on its Web site and distributes the e-mail newsletter *Freedom to Learn Online*.

United Nations Development Programme (UNDP)
One United Nations Plaza, New York, NY 10017• (212) 906-5317 Web site: www.undp.org

The United Nations was established in 1945 to, among other things, help nations cooperate in solving international economic, social, cultural, and humanitarian problems. The UNDP engages in global advocacy and analysis to generate knowledge about—and develop policies to aid—developing nations. UNDP's primary areas of interest are democracy, democratic governments, poverty reduction, environmental protection, sustainable energy, gender issues, HIV/AIDS, information and communication, technology, and crisis prevention and recovery. Numerous reports and fact sheets on these topics are available on the UNDP Web site.

Women's Alliance for Democracy in Iraq (WAFDI)
1730 Arlington Blvd., Arlington, VA 22209 • e-mail: sarbagh-salih@cs.com • Web site: www.wafdi.org

WAFDI is an international nonpartisan and not-for-profit women's rights organization. WAFDI is dedicated to a free and democratic Iraq with full and equal individual rights for women. The organization is committed to the advancement and empowerment of women in all areas of society including but not limited to family, economics, education, health, arts, literature, sports, and politics.

Bibliography

Books

Bond, Jon R., and Kevin B. Smith, *The Promise and Performance of American Democracy.* Wadsworth, 2007.

Diamond, Larry, Marc F. Plattner, and Daniel Brumberg, eds., *Islam and Democracy in the Middle East.* Baltimore: Johns Hopkins University Press, 2003.

Dunn, John, *Democracy: A History.* New York: Atlantic Monthly, 2006.

Hudson, William E., *American Democracy in Peril: Eight Challenges to America's Future.* Washington, DC: CQ, 2006.

Janda, Kenneth, Jeffrey M. Berry, and Jerry Goldman, *The Challenge of Democracy: Government in America.* Boston: Houghton Mifflin, 2006.

Mandelbaum, Michael, *Democracy's Good Name: The Rise and Risks of the World's Most Popular Form of Government.* New York: PublicAffairs, 2007.

Miroff, Bruce, Raymond Seidelman, and Todd Swanstrom, *Debating Democracy: A Reader in American Politics.* Boston: Houghton Mifflin, 2005.

Parenti, Michael, *Democracy for the Few.* Wadsworth, 2007.

Schumpeter, Jose, *Capitalism, Socialism and Democracy.* Routledge, 2006.

Sharansky, Natan, and Ron Dermer, *The Case for Democracy: The Power of Freedom to Overcome Tyranny and Terror.* New York: PublicAffairs, 2006.

Shea, Daniel M., Joanne Connor Green, and Christopher E. Smith, *Living Democracy, National Edition.* Englewood Cliffs, NJ: Prentice Hall, 2006.

Tilly, Charles, *Democracy.* Cambridge, UK: Cambridge University Press, 2007.

Periodicals

Arnold, Sebastien, "Democracy: A Universal Human Rights Pill?" *Earth Focus One Planet-One Community* Summer 2006: 25–27.

Beinart, Peter, "Is Freedom Failing?" *Time* 21 May 2007: 32.

Buckley Jr., William F., "Democracy as Spinach." *National Review*, 27 Feb. 2006: 54–55.

Chatterji, Aaron, and Siona Listokin, "Corporate Social Irresponsibility." *Democracy: A Journal of Ideas* 3, Winter 2007. < www.democracyjournal.org/article.php?ID = 6497 >.

Cheney, Liz, "Why America Must Promote Democracy in the Middle East." *ABC News* 17 Sept. 2007. < http://abc news.go.com/Politics/Story?id = 3611675&page = 1 >.

Clark, Wesley, "War Didn't and Doesn't Bring Democracy." *Washington Monthly* May 2005.

Diamond, Larry, and Joanne J. Myers, "Universal Democracy? Prospects for a World Transformed." *Carnegie Council for Ethics in International Affairs* 26 Feb. 2004. < www.cceia.org//resources/transcripts/4398. html >.

Dinh, Viet D., "How the USA Patriot Act Defends Democracy." *Foundation for the Defense of Democracies* 1 June 2004. < www.defenddemocracy.org/usr_doc/USA_ Patriot_Act_2.pdf >.

Dobriansky, Paula, "Dr. Paula J. Dobriansky, Under Secretary of State for Global Affairs, Remarks to the Baltimore Council on Foreign Affairs, Baltimore, Maryland." *U.S. Department of State* 9 Feb. 2004. < http://usinfo.state. gov/dhr/Archive/2004/Feb/11-586111.html >.

"Exporting Chaos; America Talks About Building Democracy in the Middle East. In Fact, It Fosters Mainly Violence and Failed States." *Newsweek International* 5 June 2006.

Fish, Stanley, "Shared Governance: Democracy Is Not an Educational Idea," *Change* Mar.–April 2007. < www.

carnegiefoundation.org/change/sub.asp?key = 98&s
ubkey = 2281 > .

"The Flight from Democracy," *Independent* 28 July 2007.
< http://comment.independent.co.uk/leading_articles/art
icle2811632.ece > .

Gause, F. Gregory, "Can Democracy Stop Terrorism?" *Foreign
Affairs* Sept.–Oct. 2005. < www.foreignaffairs.org/2005
0901faessay84506/f-gregory-gause-iii/can-democracy-
stop-terrorism.html > .

Holt, Pat M., "To Spread Democracy Abroad, Respect the
Law at Home." *Christian Science Monitor* 2 Feb. 2006.
< www.csmonitor.com/2006/0202/p09s01-coop.html > .

Huq, Aziz, "Who's Watching Whom?" *National Voter* Oct.
2006: 4.

Ignatius, David, "In Democracy's Name, the US Has Helped
Cede Iraq to Iran." *Daily Star* (Lebanon) 30 Aug. 2007.
< www.dailystar.com.lb/article.asp?edition_id = 10&categ
_id = 5&article_id = 84902# > .

Krastev, Ivan, "The Anti-American Century?" *Journal of
Democracy* 15. 2, April 2004: 5–16.

Krueger, Alan B., "Cash Rewards and Poverty Alone Do Not
Explain Terrorism," *New York Times* 24 May 2003: C2.

Lieven, Anato, and John Hulsman, "The Folly of Exporting
Democracy." *TomPaine.com* 12 Sept. 2006. < www.tom
paine.com/articles/2006/09/12/the_folly_of_exporting_d
emocracy.php > .

"The Limits of Democracy." *Newsweek* 29 Jan. 2007: 35.

Lindberg, Tod, "The Treaty of the Democratic Peace; What
the World Needs Now." *Weekly Standard* 12 Feb. 2007.

Marshall, Rachelle, "U.S. Effort to 'Spread Democracy'
Leaves a Trail of Conflict and Suffering." *Washington Report
on Middle East Affairs* May–June 2005: 7–10.

Ottolenghi, Emanuele, "Life and Liberty: Democracy at War."
National Review 29 July 2005. < www.nationalreview.
com/comment/ottolenghi200507290812.asp > .

Peters, Ralph, "Democracy's Global Crisis: Not the Promised Cure-All." *Real Clear Politics* 19 Apr. 2006. < www.real clearpolitics.com/articles/2006/04/democracys_global_cr isis_not_t.html > .

"Poll: Muslims Favor Democracy, If Rooted in Islamic Principles," *National Catholic Reporter* 9 Feb. 2007: 3.

"Secretary of State Condoleezza Rice at the Post," *Washington Post* 25 Mar. 2005. < www.washingtonpost. com/wp-dyn/articles/A2015-2005Mar25.htmp > .

U.S. Department of Energy, "Winning the War on Terror." 2005. < www.mbe.doe.gov/budget/05budget/content/ appendix/terror.pdf > .

Zakaria, Fareed, "A Quiet Prayer for Democracy." *Newsweek* 14 May 2007: 45.

Web Sites

Democracy Watch (www.www.dwatch.ca/). Canada's leading citizen group, Democracy Watch advocates democratic reform, government accountability, and corporate responsibility. For more than thirteen years it has won important systemic changes to key laws in Canada. Its Web site contains information on the organization's work and a thorough and thoughtful definition of democracy.

Freedom House (www.freedomhouse.org). Freedom House is a nonprofit, nonpartisan organization that works for worldwide expansion of political and economic freedom through international programs and publications. Its Web site has a plethora of reports on the state of democracy around the world.

Foundation for Defense of Democracies (www.defend democracy.org). Founded shortly after the attacks of September 11, a group of philanthropists and policy makers to support the defense of democratic societies, the Foundation for the Defense of Democracies (FDD) seeks to promote pluralism, defend democratic values, and fight ideologies that drive terrorism. Its Web site contains numerous publications on democracy based on policy research, democracy training, strategic communications, and investigative journalism.

MoveOn.org (www.moveon.org). One of the largest political action committees in the country, MoveOn.org serves as a central organizing point for Americans who want to seek a more progressive America. It conducts a variety of campaigns, including protection of democracy, civil liberties, and freedom of speech. It strives to revive democracy in America, organizing Americans and making their voices heard by legislators. Its Web site has information on MoveOn programs and platforms and advises Americans on how to get more involved in the political process.

World Movement for Democracy (www.wmd.org). A global network of activists, practitioners, academics, policy makers, and funders who promote democracy, giving practical help to those who struggle to open closed societies, challenge dictatorships, democratize political systems, consolidate emerging democracies, and strengthen established democracies. Its Web site offers information on its many programs.

Index

Picture Credits

About the Editor

Lauri S. Friedman earned her bachelor's degree in religion and political science from Vassar College in Poughkeepsie, NY. Her studies there focused on political Islam. Friedman has worked as a non-fiction writer, a newspaper journalist, and an editor for more than 8 years. She has accumulated extensive experience in both academic and professional settings.

Friedman is the founder of LSF Editorial, a writing and editing outfit in San Diego. Her clients include Greenhaven Press, for whom she has edited and authored numerous publications on controversial social issues such as gay marriage, prisons, genetically modified food, racism, suicide bombers, and the drug abuse. Much of the *Writing the Critical Essay* series has been under her direction or authorship. She was instrumental in the creation of the series, and played a critical role in its conception and development.